PERGAMON INTERNATIONAL LIBRARY
of Science, Technology, Engineering and Social Studies

*The 1000-volume original paperback library in aid of education,
industrial training and the enjoyment of leisure*

Publisher: Robert Maxwell, M.C.

Woman's Nature

THE PERGAMON TEXTBOOK
INSPECTION COPY SERVICE

An inspection copy of any book published in the Pergamon International Library
will gladly be sent to academic staff without obligation for their consideration for
course adoption or recommendation. Copies may be retained for a period of 60 days
from receipt and returned if not suitable. When a particular title is adopted or
recommended for adoption for class use and the recommendation results in a sale
of 12 or more copies the inspection copy may be retained with our compliments.
The Publishers will be pleased to receive suggestions for revised editions and new
titles to be published in this important international Library.

THE ATHENE SERIES
An International Collection of Feminist Books
General Editors: Gloria Bowles and Renate Duelli-Klein
Consulting Editor: Dale Spender

The ATHENE SERIES assumes that all those who are concerned with for-mulating explanations of the way the world works need to know and appreciate the significance of basic feminist principles.

The growth of feminist research has challenged almost all aspects of social organization in our culture. The ATHENE SERIES focuses on the construc-tion of knowledge and the exclusion of women from the process—both as theorists and subjects of study—and offers innovative studies that challenge established theories and research.

Volumes in the Series

MEN'S STUDIES MODIFIED
The Impact of Feminism on the Academic Disciplines
edited by Dale Spender

MACHINA EX DEA
Feminist Perspectives on Technology
edited by Joan Rothschild

NOTICE TO READERS

May we suggest that your library places a standing/continuation order to receive all future volumes in the Athene Series immediately on publication? Your order can be cancelled at any time.

Also of interest

WOMEN, POWER AND POLICY
edited by Ellen Boneparth

WOMEN'S STUDIES INTERNATIONAL FORUM*
A Multidisciplinary Journal for the Rapid Publication of Research Communications & Review Articles in Women's Studies
Editor: Dale Spender

Special Issues of Women's Studies International Forum available in hardcover:

WOMEN AND MEN'S WARS/Judith Stiehm

WOMEN AND ISLAM/Azizah al-Hibri

THE WOMEN'S LIBERATION MOVEMENT—EUROPE AND NORTH AMERICA/J. Bradshaw

*Free sample copy available on request

Woman's Nature

Rationalizations of Inequality

Marian Lowe
Boston University

Ruth Hubbard
Harvard University

Pergamon Press

New York • Oxford • Toronto • Sydney • Paris • Frankfurt

Pergamon Press Offices:

U.S.A. Pergamon Press Inc., Maxwell House, Fairview Park, Elmsford, New York 10523, U.S.A.

U.K. Pergamon Press Ltd., Headington Hill Hall, Oxford OX3 0BW, England

CANADA Pergamon Press Canada Ltd., Suite 104, 150 Consumers Road, Willowdale, Ontario M2J 1P9, Canada

AUSTRALIA Pergamon Press (Aust.) Pty. Ltd., P.O. Box 544, Potts Point, NSW 2011, Australia

FRANCE Pergamon Press SARL, 24 rue des Ecoles, 75240 Paris, Cedex 05, France

FEDERAL REPUBLIC OF GERMANY Pergamon Press GmbH, Hammerweg 6, D-6242 Kronberg-Taunus, Federal Republic of Germany

Second printing, 1984.

Library of Congress Cataloging in Publication Data

Main entry under title:

Woman's nature.

(Athene series)
Includes index.
Contents: Introduction/Marian Lowe & Ruth Hubbard--Social effects of some contemporary myths about women/Ruth Hubbard--Women's nature and scientific objectivity / Elizabeth Fee--[etc.]
1. Women--Social conditions--Addresses, essays, lectures. 2. Equality--Addresses, essays, lectures. 3. Feminism--Addresses, essays, lectures. 4. Rationalization (Psychology)--Addresses, essays, lectures. I. Hubbard, Ruth, 1924-   . II. Lowe, Marian. III. Series
HQ1206.W865   1983   305.4   83-4066
ISBN 0-08-030143-6
ISBN 0-08-030142-8 (pbk.)

Printed in the United States of America

Contents

CONTENTS

List of Figures

Figure

Fig. 1. Furniture Workers, Memphis, Tennessee. Photograph by Earl Dotter/American Labor.

Introduction

MARIAN LOWE
RUTH HUBBARD

This is a book about false descriptions of women's nature and about how such myths function to limit our participation in society, distort our views of ourselves, and constrain our visions and work for a better future. The authors are from a variety of ethnic and racial backgrounds, have grown up in the east, south, midwest, and west of the United States, in Central Europe, and in southeast Asia and are from working class, middle class, and professional families. Since we come from different academic disciplines in the natural and social sciences (chemistry, biology, sociology, anthropology, and the history and philosophy of science), we emphasize different aspects of our subject. But we bring our perspectives together to underline our conviction that there is no single myth of woman's nature. What people have claimed to be woman's natural behavior in fact stereotypes different groups of women differently. We try to show that the effects of these myths are varied and can express themselves in indirect and unexpected ways. We examine the role of science in the creation and reinforcement of myths about women and, conversely, the effects such myths have on science. We conclude that the concept of woman's nature (indeed, of human nature) has no scientific meaning and is not useful in struggles to achieve economic and social equality.

Unfounded generalizations about woman's nature are particularly destructive at this time when increasing numbers of women are in the wage labor force and when the women's movement has provided a voice demanding that we be treated as equals. For at the same time, powerful forces in government, business, and the country at large oppose changes in women's social and economic position, as they do other major social changes. They use ideas of woman's nature, ideas that behavior is innate and unchangeable (or at least difficult to change), to focus on limitations that they claim may be biologically inherent. These ideas restrict the framework within which scholars and policymakers view the potential for social change, and so help to counteract social change or to control it.

Many Americans, whatever their social position, believe the standard American credo that we live in a meritocracy, a land of equal opportunity for all, where ability is the primary determinant of a person's social position. Evidence of discrimination, such as racism or sexism, and inequalities of opportunity that result from it, are brushed off as localized flaws in an otherwise fair and just system that can be corrected by social reforms, such as better laws and better law enforcement. In reality, Western industrial societies are highly structured and stratified, with a few people – mostly upper-middle and upper class, white men – holding power and privilege at the top, and the large majority of people hierarchically arranged below them. White men of the working class, men of color, and women of whatever ethnic, class, and racial origins, are vastly underrepresented among those who hold power and who control the major social and economic decisions.

For the people near the top, the attractions of a belief in meritocracy should be obvious. It is in their interest not only to believe in it, but to convince those lower down of its validity, and they exert great effort to do just that. Once the meritocratic model is accepted, it is easy to believe that a particular group does badly because its members are less able or have less of what it takes for success than those higher up. Discussions and analyses of social hierarchy become limited to examining differences in the relative abilities of individuals or groups and to searching for the biological origins of these differences. The role of social inequality in generating differences or contributing to them need not be discussed.

Those who do research on sex, race, or class differences or who popularize the research in the media usually are not advocates of major social change. Not surprisingly, then, theories that root sex, race, or class differences in biology receive a great deal of publicity. To someone who really believes that this unequal social system is based on equal opportunity, a belief in biological determinism is almost inevitable. And for someone who opposes social change, it is convenient to believe that social inequality is rooted in biology. In that case, one can argue that major changes in the social and economic order would require not major political changes – which, in principle, can be brought about rather quickly – but profound changes in human biology, which are difficult to achieve and may take eons.

Inequality in our society is multidimensional. It arises from many factors and changes with time. Sex is a crucial determinant of social role, but many other factors also define an individual's position in the social hierarchy. Among them are race, age, and a number of aspects related to class, such as education, income, the type of work one does, and the range and types of choices available. A person's position in the hierarchy is the result of a complex interaction among all these factors, as well as of the social position of one's parents. Thus inequality is complex and no single, simple rationalization can adequately reflect its nature. Even the biological explanations must be modified to fit different lives.

A generalized description of woman's biological nature has been created, but when it comes to explaining the status of actual women, the picture, as we would expect, is modified. The arguments used to explain and rationalize the positions of middle class white women, working class Black women, rural Native American women, or slave women in the nineteenth century are necessarily somewhat different. However, they all somehow invoke the capacity to bear children. The universal, idealized description of the nature of women that has been constructed from this multiplicity of pictures tends to correspond quite closely to the myth of the nature of white, middle class women as passive, nurturing, and focused on motherhood and domesticity.

In this collection, we try to give a feeling for the diversity of claims about woman's nature, as well as for some common themes that run through them all. We also try to be explicit about their political nature and effects. We believe that these claims are based on the unfounded assumption that individual merit leads to success in this society, and that they draw unproved — and unprovable — connections between behavior and biology. But even though we think these claims have little scientific merit and criticize them severely, we cannot ignore them because they are politically loaded. Arguments that purport to establish the biological basis of social inequality not only constrain behavior and aspirations for social change, but can also become self-fulfilling prophesies that contribute to the behaviors and social differences that they purport to explain. Indeed, they can even help to shape the very biological differences that their advocates say they explain. Furthermore, focusing on the origins of differences in behavior between different groups is a diversion from socially pressing issues because it directs attention to the wrong questions. People find themselves debating irrelevant and unanswerable questions about the origins of behaviors, rather than deciding what we must do to change the oppressive situations in which many women live. The message of the chapters in this collection (separately and together) is that people's biological and social experiences are intimately interwoven and build upon each other in such multiple ways that it is impossible to sort them out.

There is one more point. The tradition of focusing on behavioral differences and their origins is so strong that feminists, at times, use notions of woman's nature to describe us. Some feminist theorists base their analyses on assumptions about the universal and inevitable oppression of women by men, assumptions that readily become intertwined with biological arguments about intrinsic differences between women and men. Others consider women innately superior because of traits they trace to female reproductive capabilities. We feel a special urgency to stress the fallacies and dangers of such efforts. People are social organisms, and what counts is how we function in society. That depends on our opportunities and experiences, which are continually and inextricably affected by biological and social influences. The ways that we live are conditioned by the economic, political, and social institutions into which our biology is knit. We cannot sort them out and analyze what is "natural" about our social lives. From one viewpoint, everything we do is natural: we are biological organisms, and hence everything we do and make is part of nature. But living in our steel and concrete jungles, amidst a technology that we often serve, rather than it serving us, we may think of our environment as entirely "unnatural" and antithetical to our biological make-up. Accepting this point of view and reflecting on the profound differences between our present environment and that in which our ancestors evolved and lived long ago, some people conclude that present social ills derive from incompatibilities of biology and culture. Such juxtapositions, however, are pointless. They cannot yield much socially useful information about our lives today and do not provide us with tools with which to work toward liberation and equality. To that end, our decisions and efforts must be economic and political.

Woman's Nature

Fig. II. Welders from "Good Work, Sister!" Women shipyard workers of World War II. Courtesy of Library of Congress.

1
Social Effects of Some Contemporary Myths about Women

RUTH HUBBARD

In this introductory article, Ruth Hubbard discusses the ways that myths about woman's nature are used to oppress women, pointing out some of the inconsistencies between the ideology and the reality of women's lives. She shows how the ideology that labels women as primarily reproducers has been and still is used to channel us into low paying, dead-end jobs, though these often are jobs that involve significant skills, responsibilities, and health risks.

SOCIAL MYTHS AND SOCIAL CONTROL

The dominant belief system of a society is often completely intertwined and hidden in the ordinary truths and realities that the people who live in that society accept without question. This tends to obscure the fact that these beliefs are actively generated and furthered by members of the dominant group because they are consistent with that group's interests. Further, these beliefs are intended to stabilize the social conditions that are required to perpetuate the hegemony of the dominant group. This is how we must regard present day scientific ideas about women's nature. They are part of the dominant belief system, but are myths that do not offer an accurate description of women's lives or explain the differences in the social and economic status of women and men.

Oppressive ideas and explanations that derive women's roles from women's "nature" are grounded in the material conditions in which the scientists who generate them live. These scientists are predominantly university-educated, economically privileged white men, who either belong to the hegemonic group or identify with its interests. (The few women and Third World men who have recently gained access to the scientific elite generally have the same economic and educational backgrounds as the traditional, white male members and often identify with the same interests.) It is therefore not an accident that scientists'

1

perceptions of reality, as well as their descriptions of it, often serve to perpetuate and bolster the privileges of that disproportionately small group of people who have economic and social power in society.

One way that scientific explanations have served the ends of those in power has been by "proving" that the economic, social, and political roles of members of the different classes, races, and/or other socially significant groupings within the society are consistent with their biological natures and derive naturally from them. This is the way the ideology of woman's nature functions. It provides justifications for setting limits on women's roles, activities, and aspirations that are consistent with the social needs and goals perceived by those who have power to rule the society and to generate its ruling ideas. The roles women (and men) occupy in society are thus said to originate in mother nature, rather than in the society in which we live. Internalized by women, this ideology helps to make us, too, accept our allocated roles as natural.

Although the grounding of social roles in biological differences takes a scientific form in our society, it is important to see clearly that the basis for the theories is political, not simply a matter of science gone astray. Other theories have appeared in other cultures and play similar functions there. For example, Beatrice Medicine, in chapter 4, discusses views held by the Lakota Sioux and points out the several, and sometimes contradictory ways, that notions of woman's nature are used to socialize American Indian girls to accept traditional and contemporary Native American norms, as well as Anglo ones − norms that often are oppressive, though they occasionally also acknowledge women's strengths.

Because the ideology of woman's nature plays a critical role in keeping women "in our place", in this scientific age it is important to examine scientific theories that are used to support it. Therefore I shall describe some of the ways that scientific assumptions about women's biology have led us to accept discriminatory social arrangements as appropriate and natural. Indeed, the very notion that there exists a prototypical woman who can be described in ways that reflect and have meaning for the lives of the many different women living in very different geographical, economic, political, and social settings needs to be challenged. For example, Marian Lowe shows in her chapter in this volume that naturalistic explanations of women's status in society can be quite insidious because they can affect and literally shape our biology by determining the material conditions in which we live − what and how much we eat and do, how stressful our lives are, and so on. For example, women are on average weaker than men at least partly because boys are encouraged to be more active than girls from earliest childhood, and girls are admonished to act like ladies. Thus, to some extent − though we do not know how much − the biological sex differences that are not specifically involved with reproduction reflect the different ways that girls and boys and women and men live.

WOMEN'S LIVES: MYTH AND REALITY

It is important to be aware that the ideology of woman's nature can differ drastically from, and indeed be antithetical to, the realities of women's lives. In fact, the ideology often serves as a smokescreen that obscures the ways women live by making people (including women) look away from the realities or ask misleading questions about them.

What are some of the realities? One is that women, with few exceptions, work and have always worked, though the term work has over the centuries been increasingly defined to mean what men do. Women's work is often trivialized, ignored, and undervalued, both in economic and political terms. For example, it is not called work when women "only" care for their households and children. Indeed, much of the work women do does not appear in the GNP and hence has no reality and value in standard descriptions of the economy. It is a fact that women work considerably more than men if all the work women do is counted — on average, about 56-65 hours per week as against men's 40-48 — since in addition to working for pay, most women also do most or all housework, as well as most volunteer work in schools, hospitals, and other parts of the community. Women earn 57 cents for every dollar men earn, not because we do not work as much or are less effective, but because women usually are paid less than men in work places and because much of women's work is unpaid. If women stopped doing all the work for which we are not paid, this society would grind to a halt, since much of the paid work men do depends heavily on women's unacknowledged and unpaid household labor.

The ideology that labels women as the natural reproducers of the species, and men as producers of goods, has not been used to exempt women from also producing goods and services, but to shunt us out of higher paying jobs, professional work, and other kinds of paid work that require continuity and give some power over one's own and, at times, other people's lives. Most women who work for pay do so in job categories such as secretary or nurse, which often involve a great deal of concealed responsibility, but are underpaid. This is one reason why affirmative action within job categories cannot remedy women's economic disadvantage. Women will continue to be underpaid as long as access to better paying job categories is limited by social pressures, career counseling, training and hiring practices, trade union policies, and various other subtle and not so subtle societal mechanisms (such as discouraging the interest of girls in mathematics and scientific subjects). An entire range of discriminatory practices is justified by the claim that they follow from the limits that biology places on women's capacity to work. Though exceptions are made during wars and other emergencies, these are forgotten as soon as life resumes its normal course. Then women are expected to return to their subordinate roles, not because the quality of their work during the emergencies has been inferior, but because these roles are seen as natural.

Recently a number of women employees in the chemical and automotive industries actually have been forced to choose whether to work at relatively well-paying jobs or be able ever to have children. In one instance, five women were required to submit to sterilization by hysterectomy in order to avoid being transferred from work in the lead pigment department at the American Cyanamid plant in Willow Island, West Virginia to janitorial work at considerably lower wages and benefits. Even though none of these women was pregnant or planning a pregnancy in the near future (indeed, the husband of one had had a vasectomy), they were considered pregnant or "potentially pregnant" unless they could prove that they were sterile. This goes on despite the fact that exposure to lead can damage sperm as well as eggs and can affect the health of workers (male and female) as well as a "potential fetus." But it is important to notice that this vicious choice has been forced only on women who have recently entered what had previously been relatively well-paid male jobs. Women whose work routinely involves exposure to chemical or radiation hazards in traditionally female jobs such as nurses, X-ray technologists, cleaning women in surgical operating rooms, beauticians, secretaries, workers in the ceramics industry, and domestic workers are not warned about the presence of chemical or physical hazards to their health or to that of a fetus, should they be pregnant. In other words, protection of women's reproductive integrity is being used as a pretext to exclude women from better paid job categories from which they had previously been excluded by discriminatory employment practices, but women (or, indeed, men) are not protected against health endangering work in general.(1)

The ideology of woman's nature that is invoked at these times would have us believe that a woman's capacity to become pregnant leaves her at all times physically disabled by comparison with men. The scientific underpinnings for these ideas were elaborated in the nineteenth century by the white, university-educated, mainly upper class men who made up the bulk of the new professions of obstetrics and gynecology, biology, psychology, sociology and anthropology. But these professionals used their theories of women's innate frailty only to disqualify the girls and women of their own race and class who would be in competition with them for education and professional status and might also deprive them of the kinds of personal attention and services they were accustomed to receive from their mothers, wives, and sisters. They did not invoke women's weakness to mitigate the exploitation of poor women working long hours in homes and factories that belonged to members of the upper classes, nor against the ways Black slave women were forced to work for no wages in the plantations and homes of their white masters and mistresses. Dorothy Burnham eloquently tells us about slave women's lives in Chapter 3.

Nineteenth century biologists and physicians claimed that women's brains were smaller than men's, and that women's ovaries and uteruses required much energy and rest in order to function properly. They "proved" that therefore young girls must be kept away from schools and colleges once they had begun to menstruate and warned that without this kind of care women's uteruses and ovaries would shrivel, and the human race would die out. Yet again, this analysis was not carried over to poor women, who were not only required to work hard, but often were said to reproduce too much. Indeed, the fact that they could work so hard while bearing children was taken as a sign that these women were more animal-like and less highly evolved than upper class women.

SCIENCE AND SOCIAL MYTHS

During the last decade, many feminist scholars have reminded us of this history. They have analyzed the self-serving theories and documented the absurdity of the claims as well as their class and race biases and their glaringly political intent. But this kind of scientific mythmaking is not past history. Just as medical men and biologists in the nineteenth century fought women's political organizing for equality by claiming that our reproductive organs made us unfit for anything but child-bearing and childrearing, and Freud declared women to be intrinsically less stable and intellectually less inventive and productive than men, so beginning in the 1970s, there has been a renaissance in sex differences research that has claimed to prove scientifically that women are innately better than men at home care and mothering while men are innately better fitted than women for the competitive life of the market place.

Questionable experimental results obtained with animals (primarily that prototypic human, the white laboratory rat) are treated as though they can be applied equally well to people. On this basis, some scientists are now claiming that the secretion of different amounts of so-called male hormones (androgens) by male and female fetuses produces life-long differences in women's and men's brains. They claim not only that these (unproved) differences in fetal hormone levels exist, but imply (without evidence) that they predispose women and men as groups to exhibit innate differences in our abilities to localize objects in space, in our verbal and mathematical aptitudes, in aggressiveness and competitiveness, nurturing ability, and so on.(2) Other scientists, sociobiologists, claim that some of the sex differences in social behavior that exist in our society (for example, aggressiveness, competitiveness, and dominance among men; coyness, nurture, and submissiveness among women) are human universals that have existed in all times and cultures. Because these traits are ever-present, they deduce that they must be adaptive (that is, promote human survival), and that they have evolved through Darwinian natural selection and are now part of our genetic inheritance.

In recent years, sociobiologists have tried to prove that women have a greater biological investment in our children than men, and that women's disproportionate contributions to child- and homecare are biologically programmed to help us insure that our "investments" mature — in other words, that our children live long enough to have children themselves. The rationale is that an organism's biological fitness, in the Darwinian sense, depends on producing the greatest possible number of offspring, who themselves survive long enough to reproduce. This is what determines the frequency of occurrence of an individual's genes in successive generations. Following this logic a step further, sociobiologists argue that women and men must adopt basically different strategies to maximize the spreading of genes over future generations. The calculus goes as follows: because women cannot produce as many eggs as men can sperm and, in addition, must "invest" at least the nine months of pregnancy (whereas it takes a man only the few minutes of heterosexual intercourse to send a sperm on its way to personhood), each egg and child represents a much larger fraction of the reproductive fitness a woman can achieve in her lifetime than a sperm or a child does in a man's life. From this biological asymmetry, follow female fidelity, male promiscuity, and the unequal division and valuing of labor by sex in this society. As sociobiologist, David Barash, presents it, "mother nature is sexist," so don't blame her human sons.(3)

In devising these explanations, sociobiologists ignore the fact that human societies do not operate with a few superstuds; nor do stronger or more powerful men usually have more children than weaker ones. Though men, in theory, could have many more children than women can, in most societies equal numbers of men and women engage in producing children, but not in caring for them.   But these kinds of theories are useful to people who have a stake in maintaining present inequalities. They have a superficial ring of plausibility and thus offer naturalistic justifications for discriminatory practices.

It is important to recognize that though sociobiologists have argued that we must come to understand these intrinsic biological realities so that we may bring our social arrangements into conformity with them, scientists generally have not been reluctant to tamper with nature. Scientists are proud of the technical and chemical innovations that have transformed the natural environment.   And they pride themselves on the medical innovations through which healthy women's normal biology is routinely altered by means of the pill or by surgical operations that change breast or thigh size. At present, physicians routinely intervene in the normal course of pregnancy and birth, so that in the United States one out of five births is a major surgical event – a Caesarian section.   Truly, physicians and scientists are not noted for their reluctance to interfere with nature!

Though many people would like to see less interference with normal biological functions than now occurs in this overmedicated and highly technological society, the fact is that human living necessarily involves an interplay between biological and social forces. We have no way of knowing what people's "real" biology is, because the concept has no meaning. There is no such thing as human biology in the pure. In other words, what we think of as women's biology is a political construct, not a scientific one.

However, within this constraint, it is important to recognize that we have much less solid and reliable information about how our bodies function than we could have if women asked the questions that are of importance and interest to us. For example, we do not know the normal range of women's experiences of menstruation, pregnancy, childbirth, lactation, and menopause. If women want to learn about our biology, we will have to share our knowledge and experiences of how our bodies function within the context of our lives. We must also become alert and sensitive to the ways that many of the standard descriptions of women's biology legitimize women's economic and social exploitation and reinforce the status quo.

To summarize:

- People's biology develops in reciprocal and dialectical relationships with the ways in which we live. Therefore human biology cannot be analyzed or understood in social isolation.
- Reconstructions of woman's "intrinsic" biological nature are scientifically meaningless and usually are politically and ideologically motivated.
- Scientists and physicians have asked scientific questions from a male-supremist perspective, with the conscious or unconscious intention of proving that a woman's place in society derives naturally from her biological being.
- It is important to dispel naturalistic explanations that provide biological justifications for the economic and social limitations with which women must struggle.
- We do not know much about how our bodies function within the context of our lives because the right questions have not yet been asked, nor in the right ways. It is therefore worthwhile for women to generate meaningful and important questions that can yield practical information about how to live more healthfully and productively.

NOTES

(1) This is discussed by Jeanne M. Stellman and Mary Sue Henifin in their article, "No Fertile Women Need Apply: Employment Discrimination and Reproductive Hazards in the Workplace," in, Ruth Hubbard, Mary Sue Henifin, and Barbara Fried, eds., Biological Woman - The Convenient Myth (Cambridge, Mass.: Schenkman, 1982), pp. 117-145.

(2) Several recent publications have been concerned with hormones and the brain. Up to date summaries of research can be found in Robert W. Goy and Bruce S. McEwen, Sexual Differentiation of the Brain (Cambridge, Mass.: M.I.T. Press, 1980) and in a series of review articles published in Science 211 (1981): 1263-1324. Articles intended for general readers have appeared in Quest (October, 1980), Discover (April, 1981), Newsweek (May 18, 1981), Playboy (January-July, 1982), and other magazines. Feminist criticisms of sex differences research, including research on hormones and the brain, can be found in Ruth Hubbard and Marian Lowe, eds., Genes and Gender II: Pitfalls in Research on Sex and Gender (New York: Gordian Press, 1979); Brighton Women and Science Group, eds., Alice Through the Microscope (London:

Virago, 1980); Ruth Hubbard, Mary Sue Henifin, and Barbara Fried, eds., Biological Woman - The Convenient Myth (Cambridge, Mass.: Schenkman, 1982).

(3) The investment calculus of sex differences in social and economic roles is presented in many recent publications on sociobiology. Examples are Edward O. Wilson, Sociobiology: The New Synthesis (Cambridge, Mass.: Harvard University Press, 1975), chapters 15 and 16; David Barash, The Whispering Within (New York: Harper & Row, 1979); Donald Symons, The Evolution of Human Sexuality (New York: Oxford University Press, 1979). Criticisms are included in Arthur L. Caplan, ed., The Sociobiology Debate (New York: Harper & Row, 1978) and in Ashley Montagu, ed., Sociobiology Examined (New York: Oxford University Press, 1980).

2
Women's Nature and Scientific Objectivity*

ELIZABETH FEE

Western science has been developed as a supposedly objective and neutral way of learning about nature. But Elizabeth Fee points out that science is profoundly influenced by the structure of the society in which it is done. She shows how the characteristics that are attributed to science (objective, detached, abstract) are in many ways stereotypically male. She also points out that scientific practice is part of social practice and therefore reflects the values of the larger society. Thus, we should expect a sexist society to develop a sexist science. In turn, a feminist transformation of society should lead to a transformation in the methods and content of scientific knowledge.

THE LIBERAL IDEOLOGY OF SCIENCE

The question has been posed of a possible conflict of interest between women's values and the values of science: is there such a conflict, and, if so, how will it be affected by the entrance of increasing numbers of women into the scientific professions?

If we are to accept the dominant liberal ideology of science, this question makes little sense. Science, we are told, is characterized by its objectivity, that is, by its very lack of values. Values, like feelings, political commitments, or aesthetic preferences, belong to the domain of subjectivity and of individual "bias"; the methods and procedures of scientific research are so constructed as to exclude these potential sources of error from the final product: scientific knowledge. These relationships are explored more fully in Karen Messing's chapter in this volume.

The liberal ideology of science posits man as a rational individual: "man," in confronting the natural world, is capable of creating a rational knowledge of that world through a process of testing and discarding hypotheses, and thus gradually progressing toward an ever more complete knowledge of nature. The elaborated techniques of a

---

*Earlier versions of this article have been published in the International Journal of Women's Studies, Science and Nature, the Journal of College Science Teaching, and in Science for the People.

9

Fig. III. Women Students in the Laboratory of the International Institute for Girls in Spain (1920). The Laboratory was founded by Mary Louise Foster (1865-1960), Associate Professor of Chemistry at Smith College (1908-1933). M.I.T. Historical Collection.

scientific discipline, such as controlled experimentation, the use of specific quantitative and statistical techniques, the replication of findings, and the submission of results to the collective criticism of the scientific community, are specifically intended to root out any individual eccentricities, biases, or other sources of error. It is not the subjectivity of the scientist that is seen as producing knowledge so much as the objectivity of the scientific method: subjectivity, indeed, is regarded with suspicion, as a possible contaminant of the process of knowledge production, and one which must be governed by stringent controls. In this view, it should not matter in the least whether scientists are female or male; any peculiarities or biases that might arise from the sexual identity and experience of the scientist could be potential sources of error, but these, like other sources of bias, would be eliminated in the rigorous procedures of scientific testing and confirmation of results.

If we see scientific procedures and scientific knowledge as already objective, then we cannot argue that women would bring anything new to the production of science; the admission of women to the scientific professions would be urged as a simple matter of civil rights and social justice. More positively, we might claim that if there were any residual male bias lurking within the procedures and methods of science, then the introduction of women should ensure that these possible sources of error would, in their turn, be eliminated, and a more pure objectivity result.

This view seems admirably reasonable and noncontroversial. There are, however, certain rather insistent and recurrent problems. In the first place, there is the ambiguity within the whole liberal tradition about the identity of rational "man." On the one hand, this political philosophy states that men are individuals capable of conceptualizing their self-interests and acting on them in a more or less rational manner; all individuals are in some fundamental way equivalent social atoms. There is an essential and ahistoric quality that marks all men as variants of the abstraction "man," and all their historically contingent characteristics and individual peculiarities are, in this conception, merely secondary qualities. Liberal feminism adopts this tradition and asserts that women must be included within the definition of "man," and thus, that females and males must be accorded the same individual rights and freedoms.

THE IDEOLOGY OF GENDER IN LIBERAL PHILOSOPHY

We find, however, that this conception is far from the original intention, and that the liberal ideology of rational man is actually dependent on an unstated clause: that the characteristics of "man" are actually the characteristics of males, and that rational man is inextricably bound to his less visible partner, emotional woman. In fact, the construction of our political philosophy and views of human nature seem to depend on a series of sexual dichotomies, involved in the construction of gender differences. We thus construct rationality in opposition to emotionality, objectivity in opposition to subjectivity, culture in opposition to nature, the public realm in opposition to the private realm. Whether we read Kant, Rousseau, Hegel, or Darwin, we find that female and male are contrasted in terms of opposing characters: women love beauty, men truth; women are passive, men active; women are emotional, men rational; women are selfless, men selfish – and so on and on through the history of western philosophy.(1)

Man is seen as the maker of history, but woman provides his connection with nature; she is the mediating force between man and nature, a reminder of his childhood, a reminder of the body, and a reminder of sexuality, passion, and human connectedness. She is the repository of emotional life and of all the nonrational elements of human experience. She is at times saintly and at times evil, but always she seems necessary as the counterpoint to man's self-definition as being of pure rationality. Thus, Robert J. Lifton, the psychiatrist, recently argued that male and female ways of knowing are quite distinct: the male's mode of thought is through abstract ideas and symbols far removed from organic function, while the female's pattern of thought is rooted in her "identification with organic life and its perpetuation." Woman has, he stated, the "special capacity to mediate between biology and history."(2)

THE INTEGRATION OF THE IDEOLOGY OF GENDER
INTO SCIENTIFIC THOUGHT

These ideas had long been an integral part of western philosophy, but they were rarely formulated as an explicit part of scientific theory until the mid-nineteenth century, when the first wave of the feminist movement challenged traditionally accepted ideas of female and male differences. The older aristocratic classes had depended on religious authority to legitimize social hierarchy and thus maintain social order; the new bourgeois and petit-bourgeois classes turned instead to science as the new source of authority. Social "problems" were to be subjected to scientific analysis; science, with its growing prestige, would offer a more secure foundation for the new social order than either religion or philosophy. Fundamental social issues could be safely relegated to new groups of scientific experts and thus, hopefully, removed from the turbulent arena of political struggle. Once challenged, the older philosophical constructions of gender provided the program for a variety of special scientific subdisciplines that attempted to reconstruct sex differences in terms of natural law. The distinctions between female and male were weighed and measured, explained and interpreted: scientists took over from philosophers the task of assigning to women their proper place in the social order.(3)

The uneasy relationship between liberal political philosophy and the establishment of gender as a fundamental difference between humans was then reproduced within the sciences. It is clear, for example, in the

Darwinian theory of evolution and in the subsequent history of social Darwinism. Darwin's Origin of Species was modeled on classical political economy and thus treated all animal species as made up of equivalent individuals struggling in competition with each other for survival.(4) Sex played no role in the theory of natural selection. Many liberal feminists, therefore, found in this theory a justification for their argument that women should be free to compete with men in all areas of social and economic life. Darwin, however, later developed the special theory of sexual selection in order to explain sex and race differences in his Descent of Man.(5) Although the theory of sexual selection was never well integrated with natural selection, and although the genetic theory on which it was based was quickly discarded, it did provide a model for those who wanted to argue that sexual differences were fundamental to the process of human evolution.(6) Sexual selection became the forerunner of more recent varieties of socio-biology which have sought to root the social inequalities of the sexes in genetic structure. In addition to the efforts to incorporate a fundamental sexual division into the theory of evolution, many other scientific subdisciplines have since competed in the effort to locate the essential nature of sexual differentiation. Physical anthropology, metabolic theory, neurology, psychological testing, genetics, social anthropology, psychoanalysis, endocrinology, ethology, and sociobiology have all offered different ways of structuring sexual dichotomies into nature, and different programs for the interpretation of human relationships through natural law.(7)

To summarize this section, we find that the long tradition of liberal philosophy in examining the nature of "man" has carried with it a subset of themes and theories on the nature of sex differences, and a dichotomizing of experience into two distinct and opposite categories: female and male. The sciences inherited both the general framework of liberal philosophy and also the special task of defining a place for women in the natural world. These scientists were, of course, male, just as the religious authorities and philosophers had been, but we now find an interesting development: science came to be seen as necessarily male, as an essentially masculine activity. Women had always had an important role in the reproduction of religious authority (although this role had been carefully defined as a limited and subordinate one); upper class women had been known to write and interpret political philosophy; neither religion nor philosophy was perceived as an intrinsically male endeavour. The sciences, however, have been seen as masculine, not simply because the vast majority of scientists have historically been men, but also because the very characteristics of science are perceived as sex-linked.

We find that the attributes of science are the attributes of males; the objectivity said to be characteristic of the production of scientific knowledge is specifically identified as a male way of relating to the world. Science is cold, hard, impersonal, "objective"; women, by contrast, are warm, soft, emotional, "subjective." Even the hierarchy of the sciences is a hierarchy of masculinity: as the language suggests, the "hard" sciences at the top of the hierarchy are seen as more male than the "soft" sciences at the bottom.(8) Because science as a whole is perceived as male, women in science are perceived as unfeminine. J.H. Mozans, who celebrated the achievements of hundreds of scientific women in his historical survey, Woman in Science, found it necessary to defend the womanhood of his heroines, repeatedly assuring us that these scientific women could be graceful and feminine, good house-keepers and mothers.(9) Laura Bassi was a good example: while Professor of Physics at the University of Bologna, she managed to raise twelve children.

FEMINIST RESPONSES TO THE IDEOLOGY OF GENDER IN SCIENTIFIC THOUGHT

There are several possible responses to this tradition which states that the characteristics of the sexes constitute a natural polarity, that female and male are fundamentally different, and that science is essentially masculine. One is to claim, like Mozans, that women can be both female and male: mothers and physicists. Another is to deny that there are any significant sexual differences and to discount apparent differences as the result either of discrimination or of "socialization." A third possibility is to accept the dichotomy between female and male, to promote female values as an essential aspect of human experience, and therefore to seek a new vision of science which would incorporate these values.

Some recent interpretations of female culture and its relationship to science push this theme to its ultimate moral conclusion. Susan Griffin's Woman and Nature(10) and, in a different way, Carolyn Merchant's The Death of Nature(11) have played with the identification of scientific and masculine ways of thinking: both are seen as analytic, mechanistic, controlling, exploitive, and ultimately destructive. For Griffin, the abstractions of science are bearers of man's alienation from nature and are an instrument of his alienation of woman; the two sexes simply speak different languages, and it is the women's task to rediscover their own voices, to overcome a history of female silence. For Merchant, the alienation of science dates from the mechanistic materialism of the seventeenth century which expressed the merchant capitalist's relation-ship to nature; it thus represents an historically specific form of knowledge to be transcended in the future through an alliance of feminism with ecology. Both these movements are seen as being concerned with the defense of nature against exploitation, both taking the side of mother nature against her son, the industrial engineer. Female culture is seen as cooperative rather than competitive, nurturing rather than exploitative, and oriented towards communal survival rather than individual self-interest. In a similar view, Russell Means, a major figure in the American Indian movement, has denounced all forms of "European" thought as devoid of spiritual appreciation of the natural world, and as therefore leading merely to different forms of exploitation of the earth and its natural resources.(12)

Each of these views accepts and builds on the dichotomies produced by western philosophy between nature and civilization. They find that "civilization," in the guise of scientific and technological development, has been responsible for the rape of nature and conclude that the whole tradition of modern science now endangers human survival. According to Jean Baker Miller and other feminist psychiatrists and psychologists, the male psyche, as it has been socially created in the western capitalist world, is peculiarly unable to integrate self-creative activity with a primary concern for others, since men have assigned to women the primary responsibility for affiliative ties and emotional expression.(13) This, Miller says, contributes to men's inability to organize technology for human ends and produces a scientific culture which, having cut iself off from human needs, can only be recovered for humanity through a recovery of that part of human experience which has been relegated to the female.

The radical feminist critique of science and technology thus appears to agree that there is something unfeminine about science; the problem, however, is located not in women, but in the particular character of our production of scientific knowledge. In this view, the problem is not one of making women more scientific, but of making science less masculine. When masculinity is seen as an incomplete and thus distorted form of humanity, the issue of making science and technology less masculine is also the issue of making it more completely human.

These theories confront us with a specific challenge to the idea of the objectivity of science. The distance between the knowing subject and the object of knowledge is interpreted as a measure of the alienation of man from nature; man's aim of controlling nature is taken as an egotistical and dangerous desire for domination. This view calls into question our methods of creating scientific knowledge and the assumptions on which modern science has developed, as well as the products of that knowledge: indeed, all aspects of scientific production are open to question. If we accept the radical feminist view, science itself must be transformed not simply to permit the acceptance of women, but more importantly, to conceptualize new kinds of relationships between human beings and the natural world, by overcoming an alienation between culture and nature built into our current social experience and thus into our existing forms of knowledge.

QUESTIONING SCIENCE AS A SOURCE OF AUTHORITY

The radical feminist view of science is only one of the forms in which the growing popular distrust of scientific institutions and authority is expressed. Antagonism towards established scientific authority is also found in the antinuclear and environmental movements, radical science movements, and alternative technology groups on the one hand, and in fundamentalist religious and creationist organizations on the other.(14) Whether identified with left- or right-wing political groupings, these share an opposition to the perceived elitism and authoritarianism of scientific experts, a resentment of the social power of academic and governmental elites, and a defense of alternate ideologies. All perceive the decision-making processes in science and technology as insulated from popular participation, and perceive scientific authority more as a form of power than as a source of truth. At a philosophical level, the rejection of science as a form of authority has been emphatically stated in the writings of Paul Feyerabend.(15)

There is a great deal of substance in these different forms of the rejection of scientific authority, and there is also a danger. Because science has been presented as an objective force above and beyond society, and because it has been seen as a monolithic power, it may appear that the claim of science to be the arbiter of truth must be accepted or rejected wholesale. If rejected, we seem to be left with complete cultural relativism, where no one form of the production of knowledge could claim truth status over any other. The story of Genesis would then have as much claim to validity as the theory of evolution; the decision between sexist and feminist interpretations of social arrangements would, in the absence of any mutually agreed upon criteria of validity, be quite simply a matter of political power.(16) It seems overly optimistic to suppose that a completely free marketplace of competing ideas and theories would result in the desired goal of a more human and more liberating knowledge.

We need not, however, go so far as to reject the whole human effort to comprehend the world in rational terms, nor the idea that forms of knowledge can be subjected to critical evaluation and empirical testing. The concept of creating knowledge through a constant process of practical interaction with nature, the willingness to consider all assumptions and methods as open to question and the expectation that ideas will be subjected to the most unfettered critical evaluation are all aspects of scientific objectivity that should be preserved and defended. The hope of learning more about the world and ourselves by such a collective process of knowledge production and testing is not one to be abandoned; the idea of individual creativity subjected to the constraints of community validation through a set of recognized procedures preserves the promise of progress.

The radical feminist critique of science and objectivity, therefore, needs to be developed in ways that will allow us to identify those aspects of scientific activity and ideology which need to be questioned and rejected, without at the same time abandoning the ideal that we can come to an ever more complete understanding of the natural world through a collective and disciplined process of investigation and discovery. "Science" is not monolithic; there is not, in fact, a single "scientific method"; there are many sciences and many scientific methods. The sciences are dynamic and have each undergone many shifts in their underlying assumptions and procedures; we need not suppose that even the most determined critique of currently existing science or proposals for alternate forms and visions of scientific investigation necessarily implies a rejection of either rationality or progress. The proposition that we must either accept science as it is now or collapse into mysticism and irrationalism, may be simply a tactic to discourage critical inquiry.

THE CONCEPT OF OBJECTIVITY

Let us begin with one of the central concepts in the ideology of science, the concept of objectivity. The idea of scientific objectivity is sufficiently vague to carry with it a multitude of meanings; many of these are more closely tied to the ideology of science than to the actual processes of scientific work and serve mainly to mystify scientific reality. We might see scientific production in a clearer light if these did not impede our view.

The Relationship Between the Production of Knowledge and its Social Uses

The concept of objectivity creates a hierarchy of distances within science, a series of dichotomies and silences. One of the more obvious concerns the relationship between the production of knowledge and its social uses. The idea of objectivity can be used to create a distance between the production of pure science − seen as the pursuit of knowledge for its own sake, an abstract and value-free ideal, involving purely political and economic considerations − and its uses. If the production of knowledge is isolated from the uses to which that knowledge is put, then the scientist is freed from any social or moral responsibility. Even the scientist who accepts funding from military sources is therefore free to insist that the use of "his" research is outside "his" control, and not part of "his" responsibility; the researcher in a corporate laboratory is free to consider "his" work as purely objective and unfettered by any economic considerations.

If scientists take no responsibility for the uses of science, then it is supposedly up to the general public in a democracy to monitor the social applications of scientific research. The majority, however, know little of the technical work nor of its possible implications; when community groups do become alarmed, as in the case of recombinant DNA research, they may be readily discounted as uninformed and even as "hysterical." As in the case of Three Mile Island, the problem may be formulated in terms of popular "anxiety" instead of social respon-sibility. The voices of scientific authority are more often called upon to quiet public distress than to articulate the grounds for concern; scientific expertise becomes a shield against the effort to ensure public accountability. In this context, scientists who retreat behind the screen of pure science are passively abandoning their social responsibility; those who choose to become actively involved risk being seen as no longer "objective." Here, the notion of "objectivity" becomes merely a code word for the political passivity of those scientists who have tacitly agreed to accept a privileged social position and freedom of inquiry within the laboratory in return for their silence in not questioning the social uses of science or the power relations that determine its direction.

The Relationship Between Thinking and Feeling

On a personal level, the claim of "objectivity" may be taken as requiring a divorce between scientific rationality and any emotional or social commitment.   Thinking is supposed to be completely divorced from feeling, and feeling is said to be outside the realm of objectivity. This distance between thought and feeling can again be used to insulate the scientist, as scientist, from her or his social world. The roles of scientist and of citizen are distinct, and the scientist need feel socially responsible or emotionally involved only in her or his role as private citizen.

Popular images emphasize the idea of the scientist as a man who is emotionally detached, even emotionally cold, a purely rational being. (Thus it is still difficult to accept the idea of women scientists; emotional detachment is one of the marks of masculinity.) Here again, we may be dealing with a pervasive and powerful aspect of the mythology of science rather than with the actual conditions of scientific work. Scientists, in reality, are often deeply and emotionally committed to their work, to the solution of a particular problem, or to the elaboration of a specific world view. Indeed, many scientists like to emphasize the fact that the process of scientific discovery is a deeply personal and creative activity, often characterized by apparently nonrational moments of insight or inspiration. The style of scientific communication, however, as reproduced in scientific journals, is aimed at eliminating any traces of emotional or personal involvement: the style is cold, passive, impersonal, a jargon to be learned, a respectable mask of objective detachment, an elimination of the human subject.

The concept of scientific objectivity, when used to denote the separation of thought and feeling, may be employed to devalue any positions expressed with emotional intensity or conviction; feeling becomes inherently suspect, the mark of an inferior form of consciousness. Once this hierarchy between thinking and feeling has become internalized, it is axiomatic that those identified with "thought" can justify their dominance over those identified with "feeling." Women are very used to the separation between thought and feeling, and the ways in which it can be used to reproduce relations of dominance and subordination between the sexes; it is a familiar aspect of intimate relationships. If a man can present his position in an argument as the point of view of rationality and define the woman's position as an emotional one, then we know that she has already lost the struggle to be heard; he has already won. In terms of the politics of science, this power relationship is reproduced on a social scale: the scientific experts are in the male role, while the vast majority of the population is given the female role. Everyone lacking scientific credentials can be made to feel uninformed, unintelligent, and lacking in the skills required for successful debate over matters of public policy. Those with sufficient wealth may be able to hire the scientific expertise needed to give their positions public validation, but those without wealth must bow to the superior knowledge of the experts. Knowledge can, in this system, flow in only one direction: from expert to nonexpert. There is no dialogue: the voice of the scientific authority is like the male voice-over in commercials, a disembodied knowledge that cannot be questioned, whose author is inaccessible.

The Relationship of Subject to Object

The relationship of scientific authority to the population, or of expert to nonexpert, is one of an immense and protected distance. It parallels the privileged relationship of the producer of knowledge, the subject, to the object of knowledge: the knowing mind is active, the object of knowledge entirely passive. This relationship of domination has been immensely productive in allowing the manipulation and transformation of natural processes to serve particular human ends; when transferred to the social sciences, it also serves as a justification for the attempted manipulation of human beings as the passive objects of social engineering. Women, who have already been defined as natural objects in relation to man, and who have traditionally been viewed as passive, have special reason to question the political power relation expressed in this epistemological distancing. The subject/object split legitimizes the logic of domination of nature; it can also legitimate the logic of domination of man by man, and of woman by man. If, on the one hand, the ecological crisis requires that we comprehend "man" as a part of nature, and not as a superior being above and beyond natural processes, so also the task of human liberation requires us to see science as a part of human society, determined by particular human aims and values, and not as the depersonalized voice of abstract authority. In order to be able concretely to debate the values and intentions of scientific knowledge, we must first be able to admit that these exist: thus removing the series of screens and defenses erected in an effort to deny the social content of scientific knowledge.

The Relationship of Science to Society

This raises another set of problems with the theme of scientific objectivity, the question of the social position of scientists. We are told that the production of scientific knowledge must be independent of politically motivated interference or direction. Yet we see scientists constantly testifying before congressional committees, we find scientists in law courts, and involved in disputes at every level of public policy. It is obvious that the experts take sides. It is also obvious that these "experts" are very often funded by corporate interests, and that there are few penalties for those who find that their research supports the positions of these powerful lobbies.

We may still treasure the mythology of the individual scientist, alone in "his" laboratory and isolated from mere daily concerns, wrestling with fundamental problems of the physical universe. In reality, the scientist today is a salaried employee, part of an institutional hierarchy – perhaps a small cog in a corporate research team – working on some small aspect of a problem that has probably been formulated by others. Her or his survival depends in a very concrete way on the structure of funding decisions made far from the laboratory; she or he is dependent on economic and political decisions most often beyond her or his control or influence. In what way is the average scientific worker independent of the larger political process, and how can we say that science as a whole is autonomous of social organization?

A moment's reflection shows us that the production of scientific knowledge is highly organized and is closely integrated with the structures of political and economic power. In the twentieth century, the sciences are essential in maintaining the economic, political, and military power of all developed industrial economies. The production of scientific knowledge is involved in international competition and power politics; it is naive to present the idea of scientific objectivity as though science itself were above or beyond politics. The assertion of objectivity can, however, be used to mask the actual conditions of scientific work. Because the social position of the scientist and the particular form of organization of science are supposed to be irrelevant to the knowledge produced, we may be tempted to ignore the conditions and context of scientific production.

If, however, we look at the history of science, we can begin to see more clearly the ways in which the structures of scientific production depend on the economic and political formation of the society as a whole. Our relationships to nature are socially structured and may be seen to be a product of human history. The construction of natural knowledge is a social activity; any society will attempt to generate the kinds of natural knowledge which best fulfill its social, economic, and political needs.

In the first place, the social formation determines the kinds of questions that can be posed and the tools available for answering them. Greek philosophy, or scientia, the production of natural knowledge, was divorced from the practical problems of technological production because in a slave society, the citizen-philosopher had no need to be concerned with manual labor, and the slave had no social possibility for producing formally articulated knowledge. What we know as modern science developed only with the capitalist mode of production, with the development of new kinds of practical activities and economic needs.(17) Mercantile capitalism required accurate methods of navigation; the Italian city states required the talents of a new class of engineers to develop the science of ballistics. The effort to develop more accurate cannons spurred the investigation of the laws of motion of a moving object and required the construction of a new mechanics. Mechanics, the science of moving objects, satisfied very concrete social needs, just as a new astronomy allowed the construction of new navigational tools. As capitalism matured and became concerned with techniques of production, transformations of matter became more important and the appropriate sciences were developed to deal with this new set of concerns: chemistry, metallurgy, and later, thermodynamics. Thermodynamics made possible the deliberate construction of more efficient machinery, just as the study of chemistry permitted the production of new compounds and more efficient methods of extracting raw materials for production.

The early stages of industrial production involved an active intervention in nature and the production of knowledge in a more systematic and abstract form than was characteristic of craft production. Yet the production of scientific knowledge was itself only minimally organized; not until the late nineteenth century with the accumulation of capital in large industrial enterprises were scientists deliberately and systematically employed to develop their knowledge in the direct service of industrial production. The early German chemical and electrical industries began the employment of scientists as salaried workers, whose production of knowledge led directly to new methods and techniques to be used in the service of capital accumulation. At the same time, the German research effort showed that pure research could be even more productive in terms of new industrial and military technologies than research too closely tied to immediate utilitarian ends. Science became a major social investment, to be funded by the state and reproduced in universities as well as in private corporations.

If then, we are to examine the production of scientific knowledge, we need both macro and micro studies of social organization and its relation to knowledge production. At one level, the funding and organization of science follows social priorities as established by existing relations of power; at this level, the identity of the scientist is a secondary question, not because she or he is above politics, but rather because scientists must fit into an existing political reality in which the questions and issues for research are, in large degree, established beyond the laboratory. It will be necessary to explore the role that scientists are given in the reproduction of economic and political power within the context of a class structured society in order to understand how these relationships of power lead to the production of particular kinds of knowledge and to see why certain kinds of questions are asked, while others are rendered invisible.

At the same time, scientists do have a certain autonomy in terms of the production of knowledge and have a special responsibility to examine the ways in which particular forms of research may help or hinder the project of human liberation. In terms of the specific issues discussed in this article, several steps must be taken if we are to move in the direction of a more fully human understanding of science. The first is to readmit the human subject into the production of scientific knowledge, to accept science as an historically determined human activity and not as an abstract autonomous force. If we admit that scientific activity is not neutral, but responds to specific social agendas and needs, then we can in turn begin to see how science, and scientists, might relate in a different way to social, including feminist, questions.

IS A FEMINIST SCIENCE POSSIBLE?

This modern context for the production of scientific knowledge demonstrates the difficulty of developing a specifically feminist science within our existing economic and political system. The problem of the liberation of women would first have to become a major social concern, with the necessary social resources devoted to its solution. At the moment, the production of feminist knowledge and theory depends on the energy and ideas of only a small number of women, working individually, in response to a collective social movement, but without any significant institutional or financial base. In those areas of knowledge production that are organized (or disorganized) in a similar fashion, such as history, philosophy, anthropology, and literary criticism, it has been possible for small numbers of women to have a major influence in determining new directions for research, in posing new questions, and in developing new knowledge. This is more difficult within the sciences that are more closely integrated with the reproduction of social and economic power.

At this historical moment, what we are developing is not a feminist science, but a feminist critique of existing science. It follows from what has been said about the relationship of science to society that we can expect a sexist society to develop a sexist science; equally, we can expect a feminist society to develop a feminist science. For us to imagine a feminist science in a feminist society is rather like asking a medieval peasant to imagine the theory of genetics or the production of a space capsule; our images are, at best, likely to be sketchy and insubstantial. There is no way of imagining, in advance, a fully articulated scientific theory. We are, however, free to play with ideas and to consider the criteria that a feminist science should fulfill, but we should not confuse this with the actual production of scientific theory, nor should we take our inability to imagine a fully developed feminist science as evidence that a feminist science is itself impossible.

If we begin from the previous analysis, we can say that a feminist science would not create artificial distinctions between the production and uses of knowledge, between thought and feeling, between subject and object, or between expert and nonexpert. It would not be based on the divorce between subjectivity and objectivity, but would rather seek to integrate all aspects of human experience into our understanding of the natural world.

What, you might wonder, does this mean? Let us take the doctor-patient relationship as a simple example of the required shift of perspective. We are familiar with the situation in which the patient complains, "Doctor, it hurts here," and the physician says, "Nonsense, it can't possibly." The physician has been trained to perceive objective reality according to a specific set of medical theories; if the patient's subjective experience does not fit readily into this trained perception of objective reality, then the experience must be discounted. There is really "nothing wrong," the patient is too emotional, the pain is psychosomatic, a phantom. Within scientific medicine, the patient has no recourse, no way of establishing her own pain as "real"; her subjectivity has no claim. Within medicine as currently constituted, an enormous amount of human pain is thus relegated to the shadowy realm of psychosomatic phenomena; similarly, a large proportion of healing must be attributed to the placebo effect. Indeed, physicians use the term, placebo effect for any kind of improvement in a person's condition that current medical theory cannot explain.

It would require a different kind of analysis, a different kind of investigation, to understand the kinds of pain called "psychosomatic" and the kinds of healing attributed to the "placebo effect." It would require readmitting the patient's subjectivity as a legitimate concern of medical practice and as a necessary component of healing: an admission that tends, however, to diminish the total authority of the physician. Because scientific knowledge in medicine is necessarily mediated by clinical practice and the doctor-patient relationship, many physicians are perfectly well aware of the importance of the patient as a person and of the patient's active involvement in the process of health and disease, even if they have no theoretically adequate terms in which to express this understanding.

The women's health movement, by refusing to accept the physician as unquestioned authority, and by insisting on a more active and reciprocal relationship between doctor and patient, has given a new visibility to women's actual experience and thus offers the possibility of opening up new questions that can potentially expand the boundaries of scientific knowledge within medicine. This may require changes in our understanding of what is "real," it may require a shift in the previously rigid boundaries between objective and subjective phenomena, and it may require a more serious examination of the relationship between mind and body. Such shifts and changes do not mean the collapse of medical science or the denial of everything that has been achieved by the previous paradigm, but they do offer the possibility of moving towards an expanded and more complete form of knowledge.

If all the forms of pain and illness that were previously discounted as "psychosomatic" were to be comprehended within a larger theoretical framework, our medical sciences would not be thereby diminished, but would be rendered more complete, more adequate as an understanding of human suffering. The possibility of this kind of shift within medicine suggests the possibility of expanding other forms of scientific knowledge by admitting new questions as valid and by allowing other problems to become visible. I have argued here that the manifold meanings of the concept of scientific objectivity can be used to defend against such changes. It is also possible, however, for scientists to actively seek ways of negotiating the distance established between knowledge and its uses, between thought and feeling, between expert and nonexpert, between objectivity and subjectivity.

On a broader social level, we can ask what kinds of questions might be readmitted into science by allowing the collective definition of both the problems and methodology of research. The recent history of occupational health research in the Italian factories offers an important model for the development of new forms of scientific investigation.(18)

Prior to 1969, occupational health research was done by specialists who would be asked by management to investigate a potential problem in the factory. The expert collected individual, quantifiable information from each worker by means of questionnaires, interviews, and medical records, and then statistically combined and manipulated the data to test hypotheses about the causes of the problem. The procedure was rigorously objective; the results were submitted to management. The workers were the individualized and passive objects of this kind of research.

In 1969, however, when workers' committees were established in the factories, they refused to allow this type of investigation. The new structures of direct democracy in the workplace forced a transformation in the methods of occupational health research. Now workers would collectively produce the information needed to define and solve a problem; the generation of hypotheses would be a collective, not an individual, activity. Occupational health specialists had to discuss the ideas and procedures of research with workers' assemblies and see their "objective" expertise measured against the "subjective" experience of the workers. The mutual validation of data took place by testing in terms of the workers' experience of reality and not simply by statistical methods; the subjectivity of the workers' experience was involved at each level in the definition of the problem, the method of research, and the evaluation of solutions. Their collective experience was understood to be much more than the statistical combination of individual data; the workers had become the active subjects of research, involved in the production, evaluation, and uses of the knowledge relating to their own experience.

This example shows us what overcoming the distance between objectivity and subjectivity might mean in practice. Here, the process of transmission of knowledge is not simply from expert to nonexpert but is reciprocal; the problems and issues are defined by mutual dialogue. In principle, the same kind of process could be established between scientists and any sector of the population whose experience raises specific problems for investigation.

We still have few models for visualizing what direct democracy might mean for the future of scientific research. Historical investigations of the "woman problem" have considered women as natural objects and as passive in relation to the creation of knowledge; at this stage, we can only imagine what it might mean to be the active subjects in the creation of knowledge about ourselves and the world around us. At this point, while it is necessary to argue the case for the entrance of women into the scientific professions as presently constituted, it is also important to push the epistemological critique of science to the point where we can begin to construct a clear vision of alternate ways of creating knowledge. We must use the feminist critique as a tool for seeing what it might mean in practice to liberate science from the inherited habits of thought inscribed by the previous separation of human experience into mutually contradictory realms. Overcoming the dualisms that feminists have identified as being associated with sexual dichotomies, such as the subject/object relation, may offer the prospect of a radically transformed science, one that is as yet only faintly visible as a possibility for the future.

NOTES

(1) See, for example, Caroline Whitbeck, "Theories of Sex Difference," The Philosophical Forum 5 (1973-74): 54-80; Carol C. Gould, "The Woman Question: Philosophy of Liberation and the Liberation of Philosophy," The Philosophical Forum 5 (1973-74): 5-44; Anne Dickason, "Anatomy and Destiny: The Role of Biology in Plato's Views of Women," The Philosophical Forum 5 (1973-74): 44-53.

(2) Robert Jay Lifton, "Woman as Knower," in The Woman in America, Robert Jay Lifton, ed. (Boston: Beacon Press, 1965), pp. 27-51, cited by Lois M. Magner, "Women and the Scientific Idiom: Textual Episodes from Wollstonecraft, Fuller, Gilman, and Firestone," Signs 4 (1978): 65.

(3) Elizabeth Fee, "Science and the Woman Problem: Historical Perspectives," in Sex Differences: Social and Biological Perspectives, Michael S. Teitelbaum, ed. (New York: Doubleday, 1976); Viola Klein, The Feminine Character: History of an Ideology (London: Routledge and Kegan Paul, 1946).

(4) Charles Darwin, On the Origin of Species by Means of Natural Selection, or Preservation of Favoured Races in the Struggle for Life (London: Murray, 1859).

(5) Charles Darwin, The Descent of Man, and Selection in Relation to Sex, 2 vols. (London: Murray, 1871).

(6) For an extreme example, see Patrick Geddes and J. Arthur Thompson, The Evolution of Sex (London: Walter Scott, 1889).

(7) For critiques of specific fields within science, see, for example, Donna Haraway, "Animal Sociology and a Natural Economy of the Body Politic," Signs 4 (1978): 21-60; Diana Long Hall, "Biology, Sex Hormones and Sexism in the 1920s," The Philosophical Forum 5 (1973-74): 81-96; Elizabeth Fee, "Nineteenth Century Craniology: The Study of the Female Skull," Bulletin of the History of Medicine 53 (1980): 415-433; Jill Conway, "Stereotypes of Femininity in a Theory of Evolution," in

Martha Vicinus, ed., Suffer and Be Still: Women in the Victorian Age, (Bloomington: Indiana University Press, 1973), pp. 140-154; Elizabeth Fee, "The Sexual Politics of Victorian Social Anthropology," Feminist Studies 1 (1973): 23-29; Rayna Reiter, ed., Toward an Anthropology of Women, (New York: Monthly Review Press, 1975); Carroll Smith-Rosenberg and Charles Rosenberg, "The Female Animal: Medical and Biological Views of Woman and her Role in Nineteenth Century America," Journal of American History 60 (1973): 332-356; Barbara Ehrenreich and Deirdre English, For Her Own Good: 150 Years of the Experts' Advice to Women (New York: Doubleday, 1979); and Richard C. Lewontin, "Sociobiology: Another Biological Determinism," International Journal of Health Services 10 (1980): 347-363.

(8) For a more detailed examination of the genderization of science and its relationship to psychic structures, see Evelyn Fox Keller, "Gender and Science," Psychoanalysis and Contemporary Thought 1 (1978): 409-433.

(9) J.H. Mozans, Woman in Science, 1913; reprinted with introduction by Mildred Dressesenhaus (Cambridge, Mass.: M.I.T. Press, 1974).

(10) Susan Griffin, Woman and Nature: The Roaring Inside Her (New York: Harper & Row, 1978).

(11) Carolyn Merchant, The Death of Nature: Women, Ecology, and the Scientific Revolution (San Francisco: Harper & Row, 1980).

(12) Russell Means, "Fighting Words on the Future of the Earth," Mother Jones (December, 1980): 22-38.

(13) Jean Baker Miller, Toward a New Psychology of Women (Boston: Beacon Press, 1976). See also, Dorothy Dinnerstein, The Mermaid and the Minotaur: Sexual Arrangements and the Human Malaise (New York: Harper & Row, 1976).

(14) For the creationist antagonism towards scientific authority, see especially, Dorothy Nelkin, Science Textbook Controversies and the Politics of Equal Time (Cambridge, Mass.: M.I.T. Press, 1978).

(15) For example, Paul Feyerabend, Science in a Free Society (London: New Left Books, 1978).

(16) See Hilary Rose's attack on several of the themes of the radical science movement, "Hyper-Reflexivity – a New Danger for the Counter-Movements," Sociology of the Sciences 3 (1979): 277-289.

(17) On the Scientific Revolution, see J.D. Bernal, Science in History Volume 2: The Scientific and Industrial Revolutions (Cambridge, Mass.: M.I.T. Press, 1954); Boris Hessen, "The Social and Economic Roots of

Newton's Principia," in Science at the Crossroads (London: Cass, 1931); Edgar Zilsel, "Problems of Empiricism," in The Development of Rationalism and Empiricism (Chicago: University of Chicago Press, 1968); and Lewis Mumford, The Myth of the Machine: The Pentagon of Power (New York: Harcourt Brace, Jovanovich, 1964). For a discussion of the sexual metaphors and ideology involved in the scientific revolution, see Carolyn Merchant, The Death of Nature. For an alternative exploration of the sexual ideology of Baconian science, see E.   Fox Keller, "Baconian Science: A Hermaphroditic Birth," The Philosophical Forum 11 (1980): 299-308.

(18) For a more extended discussion of this example, see Giorgio Assennato and Vicente Navarro, "Workers' Participation and Control in Italy: The Case of Occupational Medicine," International Journal of Health Services 10 (1980):   217-232. See also Vicente Navarro, "Work, Ideology and Science, the Case of Medicine," International Journal of Health Services 10 (1980): 523-550.

Fig. IV. Cotton Picker, age 10, Bolivar County, Mississippi. Photograph by Earl Dotter/American Labor.

3
Black Women as Producers and Reproducers for Profit

DOROTHY BURNHAM

Ideas about woman's nature are often myths developed to explain and rationalize the specific circumstances in which women live. For women in different situations, these myths vary. In this article, Dorothy Burnham first outlines some major aspects of the lives of Black slave women in the United States and examines their position as workers and reproducers in the economy of slavery. She then shows how those who reaped the benefits of slavery could do so with clear consciences by accepting descriptions of their slaves as innately inferior—descriptions elaborated by respected scientists of the time.

The dominant myth of woman's nature is generally one appropriate for the lives of middle and upper class white women. By the nineteenth century, this ideology portrayed women as fragile and delicate creatures whose lives were centered around motherhood and whose bodily functions were dominated by their reproductive organs. Women were thought to be lower on the evolutionary scale than men, with a less-developed nervous system and lower intelligence. Blacks also were seen as less developed in evolutionary terms than whites. They were claimed to be more emotional and childlike and less civilized and intelligent. These two threads were brought together to create a myth, described by Burnham, that justified the position of Black slave women as "breeding women" and was used to reproduce and extend slavery. And, although this myth has been modified with time, many of its elements are still with us.

In the recurring examinations of the situation of the slave family in the United States, more and more information about the life of the Afro-American woman under slavery has come to light. The life of every slave, whether captured in Africa or born under slavery in the United States, was completely circumscribed by the demands of the market. The slave woman's productive life was determined not only by her contribution in the field and in the master's household, but also by her reproductive capacity. The circumstances of her life were shaped inexorably by the slavocracy's drive for profit.

Information about women slaves comes to us from slave narratives and the oral history of exslaves, from plantation records and slave traders, from abolitionists and antislavery people, and from observers and travelers in the South. Most of the material is so filled with disaster and tragedy that it is difficult for a Black woman like myself to be dispassionate. I will, therefore, have to leave the stark objectivity to the econometricians. Let them measure the cabin floors and the pecks of flour, and interpret the motives which they say must have driven the slave owners to take care of their female slaves in a manner that compared favorably with care given other women workers in America.

Exploitation of Afro-American women began with the Atlantic slave trade. The profits of the overseas slave trade were determined by the numbers of slaves the merchants were able to sell and the prices paid. Demands and prices, of course, for young, able, and healthy African males were the highest. Although some of the early planters must have thought of profits to be gained from the reproductive capacity of the women, it is evident that they thought a new crop of slaves could be produced by a few women. At any rate, the drive for maximum profits resulted in a severe numerical imbalance between the male and female slaves imported to the West Indies and the colonies. The earliest documents of the slave traders reflect the imbalance in importation of slaves. Catterall cites a document of 1536 in which the trader contracts to carry 4,000 slaves to the West Indies over a period of 4 years, of which one-third were to be women.(1) And a century later a letter to Philip III, King of Spain, quoted in Eric Williams, Documents of West Indian History, asked for the same proportion of import. In order to develop the production of cacao in Trinidad, Dr. Merva requests "300 pieces of slaves should be sent to that island of whom two thirds should be men and one third women."(2)

Examining the records of the Liverpool slave vessels much later, Clarkson also found "a disproportion of the sexes, there being upon the average about 5 males imported to 3 females."(3)

This imbalance was felt much more critically in the West Indies. The birth rate of the slave population never reached the level expected by the planters. Overwork and disease among the women were given as causes for the low birth birth. And as late as the eighteenth century, according to Brady and Jones, male slaves in the West Indies outnumbered the women by six to one.(4)

The early colonial records did not enumerate people by sex, so it is difficult to trace this imbalance in the United States. Figures for South Carolina, however, indicate that the proportion of men to women slaves was five to three in 1703.(5)

The 1820 census, which was the first in which the male and female populations were counted separately, still reflects greater numbers of slave men than women for the United States population as a whole. It was not until the 1840s and 1850s that a near balance of male and female slaves was achieved in the nation. Of course, there were continuing imbalances in various parts of the country and on individual plantations due to the ability of slave owners to control the movement of the slave population to suit the demands of the market. Phillips, assessing a plantation owned by Palfrey, remarked: "Its 32 men were badly proportioned to 12 women and five children [in 1811] ."(6)

Sutch's research into the period of the 1850s internal slave trade reveals further information not only about the separations forced upon the women slaves by the trade, but about the continuing regional imbalances and the consequent misery forced on the victims. He says:

> The sexual distribution of exported slaves is also suggestive. We would expect the slave breeder who did not respect the custom of monogamous sexual relations for his slaves to sell more men than women. Consistent then with the suggestion that the exporting states had a greater tendency to breed slaves than the buying states is the fact that 7% more males than females were

exported. Males were in excess among exports by 14.3% in the age class 20 to 49. Among those slaves who were 20-29 in 1850 and 30-39 ten years later, 29.8% more males than females were exported.(7)

The effect of removing millions of men in the prime of life from the African homeland over the four centuries of the Atlantic slave trade was so devastating that the conquest of the continent by the European invaders was greatly facilitated. Since there are few direct records from women slaves one can only imagine what it was like for them. In the West Indies, not only was the Black male slave population overwhelming, but the white male population was also considerably greater. The incidence of sexual exploitation, assault, and rape must have been enormous against slave women completely unprotected by law and with their cultural social protection stripped away. In the American colonies as well as in the West Indies, the loss of a balanced community, of love, and of a stable male/female relationship were the lot of generations of Black women.

The original imbalance, of course, reflected the fact that traders were paid more for male slaves. However, from the beginning plantation owners, like good husbandmen, planned on having their women slaves reproduce the stock. And they expected to do this not only with God's help, but with his blessing. In 1645, George Downing wrote to John Winthrop:

> I believe they have bought this year no less than a thousand Negroes, and the more they buy, the better able they are to buy, for in a year and half they will earn (with God's blessing) as much as they cost . . . and in short time [you will] be able, with good husbandry to procure Negroes out of the increase of your own plantation.(8)

In order to ensure their income from the children of the slave women, the slaveholding class saw to it that the laws of the colonies confirmed this right. In 1662, the Virginia assembly passed the statute which said in part:

> Be it therefore enacted and declared by this present grand assembly, that all children borne in this country shall be held bond or free only according to the condition of the mother.(9)

In the years following, other colonial legislatures enacted similar statutes. Maryland, however, in 1664 fixed the condition of children after that of their fathers. Rose comments:

> The intention of the law was apparently, to discourage the mating of white women with Negro slaves. . . . But the policy of following the paternal line was soon dropped, because by its terms the free mulatto population developed at the same rate

that white men impregnated slave women. Thus rapidly did an important fundamental of English law give way before the combined force of racial antipathy, sexual license, and the need for an exploitable labor force in the new plantation country.(10)

Accordingly, the price of the woman slave was based not only on her value as a field hand or household slave, but also on the possible value of her children of the future.

Conneau, who wrote of his experience as a slave trader in the early part of the nineteenth century, noted that a deduction of 20% was made when the woman was over 25 years, "but if young and well built with favorable appearances of fecundity, they commanded a price equal to a prime man."(11)

In their correspondence and notes to the overseers, planters often expressed their hope and reliance on the reproductive capacity of their female slaves to bring them greater wealth.

Planter Taitt complained:

Our loss of little negroes has been great the past years, but I hope it will not happen again. Let us feed, clothe and house them well and I do not fear, but they will increase rapidly.(12)

Conrad and Meyer in a 1958 study of the economics of slavery calculated the rate of return on the female slave, including field returns from her and her children's work, and the sale of her children. They concluded that the average return rate for a mother bearing five children was 7.1%; if she bore 10 children it was 8.1%.(13)

That the planters considered the children as part of the increase of their estates is reflected in the wills filed by the planters leaving unborn slave children to their heirs. Catterall cites the 1771 will of Micajah Woody, who willed to his daughter, Agatha, the first negro child that his negro woman, Beck, raised,

showing that he considered the progeny of Beck whom he knew to be a young breeding woman, as one of the means of providing for his children.(14)

Catterall also cites maternity prizes offered to stimulate Black women to produce children – one planter offering the slave woman freedom if she produced one slave child for each of his heirs.(15)

There seems to be little controversy over the fact that planters considered the fruits of reproduction to fall on the positive side of their ledger. However, there is a continuing argument over the internal slave trade and especially over allegations of deliberate breeding of slaves for the southern market.

The planters for the most part wished to project an image of a paternalistic lord presiding over a manor peopled by semi-savage Black slaves whom they were helping to civilize and teaching the art and morality or hard work. They tried desparately to separate themselves from the brutal, materialistic slave trader and the open and unconcealable cruelty of the market, to the extent of denying and having the writers of the period claim for them that they had nothing to do with breeding and raising slaves for the market. Yet the evidence seems to say that indeed the children of slave women were bred and raised in Virginia for sale in Mississippi and Alabama. The collective memory of the exslaves of Virginia, Maryland, and Delaware, as revealed in the slave narratives, is that of separation. The exslaves repeatedly relate stories of partings from brothers, sisters, and mothers sold South.

Professor Thomas Dew, who argued strongly for the slavery point of view, said in 1831:

> the slaves in Virginia multiply more rapidly than in most of the southern states, the Virginian can raise cheaper than they can buy, in fact it is one of their greatest sources of profit. . . . Virginia is in fact a Negro raising state for other states. She produces enough for her own supply and six thousand for sale.(16)

The population shifts noted by many authors also support the autobiographical stories told by exslaves. A.A. Taylor made a study of the movement of Negroes from the east to the gulf states:

> The extension of the cotton culture in the more southern states, the increased exportation of cotton, the advancing profits therefrom, the development of large sugar plantations in Louisiana, and the decreased average working life of the slave created among the planters of this region an extraordinary demand for slave labor. . . . The African slave trade, moreover, had been legally suppressed thus rendering the seaboard and other border the sole legal source.(17)

The apologists for slavery have claimed that this movement of slaves was mainly of family groups. However, observers like Olmstead and William Wells Brown and others commented on the separated children and men and women in the slave coffles. And Sutch in his study noted:

> [The] pattern of exports across age categories reveals that slaves between 15 and 39 in 1860 were exported out of the selling states at a much higher rate than slave children or the elderly. This implies that the slaves were not primarily exported in family units complete with their children and their parents. Rather it appears that a substantial exportation of young adults without children or parents took place.(18)

So the pattern of forced separation of families and communities that had begun on the coast of Guinea centuries before was continued right down to the end of the antebellum period.

Listen to the lament of Lydia Adams, a slave who had escaped to Canada:

> I am seventy or eighty years old. I was from Fairfax county, Old Virginia. I was married and had three children when I left there for Wood County where I lived twenty years. Thence to Missouri, removing with my master's family. One by one they sent four of my children away from me, and sent them to the South, and four of my grandchildren all to the South but one. My oldest son, Daniel — then Sarah — all gone. "It's no use to cry about it", said one of the young women, "she's got to go".(19)

In order to live with themselves in the face of the cruelties, the theft of life, and the tragedies the system imposed, the slavocracy and those who supported it had to invent the mythology of an inferior people: in most ways African men and women were not men and women like themselves, but something closer to animals.

As they cynically counted on the children of their slave women to support them and their legal children in luxury, they taught themselves and their children to think of these women as animals. Reverend Turner, boasting of his prosperity, for example, writes:

> I keep no breeding woman nor brood mare. If I want a Negro, I buy him already raised to my hand and if I want a horse or a mule, I buy him also.(20)

One planter's advice to his brother planter was:

> You are apprised, I suppose, that Negroes from the North have to be favored the first year. Like Kentucky mules, they have to be moderately worked, carefully treated, etc.(21)

And from Catterall's judicial cases:

> The intestate left at his death a female slave, named Bet, and a mare named Pol . . . the wench had 2 children . . . the mare died . . . having had 3 colts.

Apparently the dispute was over ownership of the colts and slave children. The learned court's decision reflects the ideology of the slaveholding class. It was: "The young of slaves stand on the same footing as other animals. . . . This increase is the product of the intestate's personal estate."(22)

In this period the court documents and journals spoke of the taint of African blood, the odious circumstances of color, the degradation of the inferior race. A judge in settling a case of whether a mulatto could testify in court, for example, answered:

It is certainly true as laid down by the presiding judge, that every admixture of African blood with European or white is not to be referred to the degraded class.(23)

The judge's remarks in another court case illustrate further how deeply the ideology of racism had settled in by 1832.
A white woman had a mulatto child after 5 months of marriage to a white man. The judge said:

The court is entirely sensible of the peculiar character of this case produced by the odious circumstances of color. . . . The stigma in our state of society is so indelible, the degradation so absolute and the abhorrence of the community against the offender and contempt for the husband so marked . . . that the court has not been able without a struggle to follow those rules which their dispassionate judgement sanctions.(24)

The racist assault on the humanity and personhood of the African woman slave took many forms. There were insulting references to her appearance. Her black skin color was referred to disparagingly, and there were learned scientific discussions over whether her hair was made of wool. Every African feature was laughed at and caricatured. Offensive and pejorative names such as pickaninny, nigger, and wench were a part of the common vocabulary and found their way into American literature.
And those who were guilty of stealing women, their services, their children, and their homelands, examined the blood lines of the slaves and determined that there was a genetic factor in their alleged propensity for rascality.
The ideological assault of the scientific community on Afro-American men and women supported the racist mythology. DeBow's Review published article after article written by academics and medical persons aimed at establishing the inferiority of the intelligence of the slaves. For example, one article by a Dr. Cartwright claimed that a defect in the

atmospherization of the blood conjoined with a deficiency of cerebral matter in the cranium . . . led to that debasement of mind which has rendered the people of Africa unable to take care of themselves.(25)

As for the continuing sexual exploitation and abuse of the woman slave, there was also at hand a convenient, valid, and moral explanation. Chancellor Harper, a judge who had served in the United States Senate, addressed The Society for the Advancement of Learning of South Carolina on the subject of the Negro:

English women of this class [prostitutes] or rather girls, for few of them live to be women die like sheep with the rot; so fast that soon there would be none left, if a fresh supply were not obtained equal to the number of deaths. . . . In such communities the unmarried woman who becomes a mother is an outcast from society and though sentimentalists lament the hardship of the case it is justly and necessarily so. . . .

After this introduction, Harper gets to the heart of his argument, for he is definitely not lamenting the cause of the British fallen women, but rather building a case for the prostitution of the female American slave.

For [the unmarried slave] is not a less useful member of society than before. . . . She has not impaired her means of support, nor materially impaired her character or lowered her station in society. She has done no injury to herself or any other human being. . . . Her offspring is not a burden, but an acquisition to her owner. . . . The creator did not intend that every individual should be highly cultivated morally and intellectually.

To cap this morality lesson, the author extols the purity of the white southern woman:

And can it be doubted that this purity is caused by and is a compensation for the evils resulting from the existence of an enslaved class of more relaxed morals.(26)

Then, as now, the exploiters had no difficulty finding people with first class credentials to advance the ideology and mythology of racism.

I have presented the third part of this chapter because the ideology of racism was an important and integral part of the building and maintaining of the slave system. As one judge admitted:

If no such condition of inferiority should become established by the general practice of nations, the law of nations must be held to be the same in respect to all races of men.(27)

Those who caused the life-long suffering of our slave mothers have long departed. The slave pens on the Guinea Coast and the slave markets in Louisiana are now museums – the painful reminders of our history. What remains for us to deal with is the cesspool of racist doctrines that persist, threatening the lifedreams and hopes of our daughters and granddaughters. There are still those today who speak in support of biological determinist theories which allege the natural inferiority of Black people.

But as we ask how they dare to insist on conducting research and publishing racist material in the name of academic freedom, history provides the answer.   Lydia Adams, born in Fairfax County, Old Virginia, gave up four children and four grandchildren for the profit of the slave system. And all concerned could justify their actions because

Professor Dew, Professor DeBow, Chancellor Harper, and Dr. Cart-wright had said that it was all right; that she and her children deserved to be robbed of their labor, abused and exploited sexually, deprived of their loved ones. For, they said, she was by nature ignorant, sensual and ugly, and incapable of being civilized.

NOTES

(1) Elizabeth Donnan, Documents Illustrative of the History of the Slave Trade to America (Washington, D.C., 1930-35), I: 16.

(2) Eric Williams, Documents of West Indian History 1492-1655 (Trinidad, W.I.: PNM Publishing Co. Ltd., 1963), I: 144.

(3) Thomas Clarkson, Abolition of the African Slave Trade (Philadelphia: James Parker Publishers, 1808), I: 45.

(4) Terence Brady and Evan Jones, The Fight Against Slavery (New York: W.W. Norton, 1977), p. 39.

(5) Peter H. Wood, "Demographic Patterns in South Carolina," in Engerman and Genovese, eds., Race and Slavery in the Western Hemisphere. Quantitative Studies (Princeton, NJ: Princeton University Press, 1974), p. 135.

(6) U.B. Phillips, Life and Labor in the Old South (Boston: Little, Brown & Co., 1963), p. 292.

(7) Richard Sutch, "The Breeding of Slaves for Sale," in Engerman and Genovese, eds., Race and Slavery, 181.

(8) Eric Williams, Documents of West Indian History, p. 292.

(9) Willie Lee Rose, A Documentary History of Slavery in North America (New York: Oxford University Press, 1976), p. 19.

(10) Ibid., p. 24.

(11) Capt. Theophilus Conneau, A Slaver's Log Book (Englewood, NJ: Prentice-Hall, 1976), p. 11.

(12) U.B. Phillips, Life and Labor in the Old South, p. 22.

(13) Alfred H. Conrad and John R. Meyer, "The Economics of Slavery in the Ante-Bellum South," Journal of Political Economy 66 (April 1958): 109.

(14) Helen H. Catterall, Judicial Cases Concerning American Slavery and the Negro (Washington, D.C., 1926-1937), I: 131.

(15) Ibid., pp. 151, 159.

(16) Thomas R. Dew, Review of Debate in Virginia Legislature of 1831 on Abolition of Slavery (Westport, CT: Negro University Press, 1970), pp. 49, 55.

(17) A.A. Taylor, "The Movement of Negroes from the East to the Gulf States from 1830-1850," Journal of Negro History 8 (1923): 373.

(18) Richard Sutch, "The Breeding of Slaves," p. 181.

(19) Richard Drew, The Refugee: A North-side View of Slavery (Reading, MA: Addison Wesley, 1968).

(20) U.B. Phillips, Life and Labor in the Old South, p. 173.

(21) Ibid., p. 277.

(22) Helen H. Catterall, Judicial Cases, II, p. 293.

(23) Ibid., p. 346.

(24) Ibid., p. 63.

(25) Cartwright, "Diseases and Peculiarities of the Negro," in J.D.B. Debow, Industrial Resources of the United States (New York: D. Appleton & Co., 1854), II: 316.

(26) Harper, "Memoir on Negro Slavery," in J.D.B. Debow, Industrial Resources, II, pp. 219, 220.

(27) John Codman Hurd, Laws of Freedom and Bondage in the United States (Boston: Little Brown, 1858-62), p. 166.

4
The Dialectic of Biology and Culture*

MARIAN LOWE

The idea that the origins of differences in human behavior and social position lie in biological differences is widely touted and has the effect of discouraging efforts to achieve social equality. The opposite point of view, that biological differences may in part arise from behavioral or social differences, has had little attention, although it has important implications for visions of alternative futures. Marian Lowe looks at some possible interactions between women's biology and our social behavior.

Although male dominance is no longer an explicit ideal of North American culture, our society still has very definite ideas about sex-appropriate behavior. In spite of the entry of large numbers of women into the wage labor force and the changes brought about by the women's movement, "masculine" and "feminine" behavior remain highly stereo-typed. These stereotypes have far-reaching effects, for ideas about appropriate behavior for women and men act as powerful constraints on how people behave and can easily become self-fulfilling prophecies. Most aspects of social life are affected, from the kinds of work considered appropriate to the details of social relationships. Because sex roles are so deeply imbedded in our social structures, the maintenance of these roles is important if social change is to be avoided or at least controlled by those with political and economic power. At present, it seems to be of particular importance to those in power that women's primary role in the rearing of children be maintained and reinforced. The re-emergence of theories claiming that sex roles, particularly women's role as nurturer, have a biological basis must be seen in this light. Such theories act as important means of creating and justifying sex role stereotypes and of opposing change.

---

*This is a somewhat modified version of a paper entitled "Social Bodies: The Interaction of Culture and Women's Biology" appearing in <u>Natural Woman - The Convenient Myth</u>, R. Hubbard, M.S. Henifin and B. Fried, eds. (Cambridge, MA: Schenkman, 1982).

Figure V. United Mine Workers, Buchanan County, Virginia. Photograph by Earl Dotter/American Labor.

However, the effects of sex-role stereotyping can go beyond molding behavior and social roles, for biology as well can be modified by the imposed constraints. In part, we may literally be shaped by our social roles. This way of looking at the relationships among biology, societal norms, and people's behavior is in sharp contrast to the usual picture drawn by biological determinists, which portrays sex roles as the products of biologically determined differences between women and men.

Current theories based on such assumptions – for example, sociobiology – do not claim that sex differences in behavior are completely determined by biology but speak of "propensities" or "predispositions" for certain behaviors depending on one's sex.(1) While somewhat less rigidly deterministic than their nineteenth century antecedents, such modern theories continue to assume that innate biological differences lurk underneath it all. As various critics have pointed out, there are a number of difficulties with these theories,(2) perhaps the most fundamental being that a great many aspects of biological function, including body size and strength, hormone levels and possibly, brain development can be changed considerably by changes in the environment.

When considering the origins of sex differences in behavior, it is important to acknowledge the extent that women and men grow up and live in radically different social environments in American culture (and in most other contemporary societies). The games we play as children, the kinds of work we do, our physical environments, the way we spend our leisure time, relationships with other people, and many other aspects of life differ greatly for women and men. At present the environments of some women are in a period of rapid change. In many cases these changes expose women to work and life experiences that are much more like those traditionally seen as appropriate for men. This is true for women entering such male dominated fields as medicine, law, science, coal mining, heavy construction and athletics. As women's environments and activities become more like men's, both in our society and others, the extent of many sex differences decreases: spatial visual ability, some measures of aggression, and a number of other behavioral traits have become more alike in women and men.(3) And as we will see, so have a number of biological traits such as size and strength. We do not know how much of the remaining sex difference in any particular trait may be due to inborn factors or to still existent environmental differences. Certainly there is no reason to suppose that the remaining differences in behavior and biology are due only to innate factors.

SEX DIFFERENCES IN STRENGTH
AND PHYSICAL PERFORMANCE

A great many cultures, including our own, assume that there are fairly substantial innate sex differences in body form that explain why men generally show superior performance on tasks reflecting strength or athletic ability. Such assumptions have powerful personal and social consequences. The ways we view our bodies constitute a basic part of our self-identification as feminine or masculine. Women and men have different expectations about physical capabilities and try to shape our bodies according to different standards of health and beauty. The assumption that women cannot do anything that requires strength powerfully reinforces social roles, while at the same time producing some of the actual strength differences. Stereotypes about strength for example, have not only affected women's participation in various sports and physical activities, but also the kinds of exercise and jobs seen as suitable.

The United States wage labor force is highly segregated by sex. This economically important division of work into women's and men's jobs is rationalized in part by ideas about innate differences in strength between the sexes. Even though many women work at jobs where a great deal of strength is needed (such as nursing, which involves the lifting of sick and sometimes obese adults), the image of the fragile female is still used to keep women out of various higher paying occupations, such as construction work or heavy industry. This is only one example of the fact that a smaller, frailer female frame is seen not only as consistent with women's social role and lack of social power, but as one of the reasons for it.(4) However, the idea that physical differences in strength can be used to explain differences in social position is clearly erroneous. Most "male" occupations, particularly those with prestige and power, such as corporate executive, politician, doctor, or army officer, do not require physical strength. In general, jobs that involve physical labor, such as digging ditches or construction work, tend not to be highly valued in our society. (The "jobs" held by a few highly paid male athletes are among the few exceptions to this rule.) In spite of this reality, men's presumed greater innate physical strength has come to be a symbol of greater male social power.(5)

Not only have sex differences in strength had little to do with causing the current sexual division of labor, but the origin of these differences is also open to question. There is growing evidence that differences in physical strength could come as much from differences in life experience as from innate factors. For sex differences in strength and other physical abilities, just as for sex differences in behavior, the relative contributions of environment and biology turn out to be impossible to pry apart. After all, not only are women's and men's biologies different, but sex differences in social roles result in major differences in the ways we use our bodies. From earliest childhood, the activities that are encouraged for girls and boys are different. Little girls are admonished to "act like a lady"; to move, speak, and think like a "lady" is not without biological effects on our shape, strength,and other abilities. Studies have indicated that, beginning at birth, parents exercise the limbs of their baby boys more frequently and vigorously than they do their girls'.(6) Later on, girls and boys are channeled into different kinds of play, with the result that many girls are involved in more sedentary activities. In adult life the earlier patterns tend to continue, although we are now seeing some changes.

In examining possible origins of sex differences in size and strength, it is helpful to look first at some of the sex differences that presently exist in the United States and other Western societies and then at the changes that occur when women's activities become more similar to men's. In discussing these differences, it is important to keep in mind that we are always comparing average values. All traits vary widely for each sex, so that differences between groups are usually smaller than the variations within each group. Overlaps between women and men are found in the distributions of most traits, except for the anatomical and physiological differences directly involved in reproduction. With this in mind, let us see what the norms are for some physical traits. On average, American men are about 5 inches taller than American women.(7) Men are heavier and more muscular. Women have a higher proportion of body fat: the average for women is 23%; the average for men, 15%.(8) Body fat is also distributed somewhat differently. For women, more of it is found around the hips and the breasts. Women have somewhat smaller, less dense bones than men. This, combined with the higher proportion of fat, means that a woman on the average weighs less than a man of the same height. Other than lighter bones, the only established skeletal differences seem to be the slightly wider pelvis and slightly shorter legs of women relative to the length of their trunk. There is no evidence for differences in elbows or shoulder joints, despite the explanation usually given as to why girls cannot properly throw a football or a baseball.

Another difference is in sweat production.(9) The Victorian adage, "A horse sweats, a man perspires, but a lady only glows," seems to have some truth in it. A woman's body temperature must be 2 or 3 degrees higher than a man's before she begins to sweat, though experts disagree as to whether this means that women are more or less heat tolerant than men. A number of other physiological differences between the sexes also may affect relative abilities to perform physical activities. These include relative numbers of red blood cells, energy utilization, and capacity to carry oxygen from the lungs to the tissues.(10)

Differences in performance also clearly exist, but they do not correspond exactly with the stereotypes.(11) In measures of strength, it appears that, overall, women are about two-thirds as strong as men. However, the degree of difference varies with muscle group. It is greatest for arm, chest, and shoulder muscles and least for the legs. Part of the difference is due to the fact that men are larger. When strength is compared for people of equal weight, the difference becomes smaller, with women about three-quarters as strong as men of the same weight. When allowance is made for sex differences in body fat and hence in muscle mass for equal weights, the differences in strength become even smaller; leg strength per unit of lean body weight actually is slightly greater for women than for men.(12)

In competitions requiring power and speed, both of which depend on strength, women's records consistently lag behind men's. Trained men perform better in events such as sprints, medium distance running or swimming, discus throwing, shot putting, and in various jumping events. In some of these, the difference in performance appears to be due primarily to sex differences in size. For the high jump and long jump, for instance, performances are essentially the same for women and men when corrected for body weight. In others, women's performances are lower even on an equal weight basis. However, in athletic events that are primarily tests of endurance, such as supermarathons (50 or 100 mile runs) or long distance swimming, women are beginning to out-perform men.(13) One theory is that in endurance events, fat as well as carbohydrate (glycogen) becomes an important source of energy, and women may be better at utilizing their stored fat. Women distance runners do not seem to experience the phenomenon known as "hitting the wall" — the point at which all the muscle glycogen is used up, which seems to occur at around 20 miles for male marathoners.(14)

Clearly, there are significant sex differences in body shape, physiology, and functioning. The question of interest here is to what extent these differences have been created and hence can be modified by environmental factors and social changes.

CHANGES IN MUSCULAR DEVELOPMENT AND STRENGTH

A Science News survey of research on sex differences in strength suggests that stereotypes about inherent female and male body types may need to be revised.

> Several researchers have concluded that much of this difference in strength is the result of society's encouraging the average man to be more active than the average woman. They feel that the social influences are so great that inherent physiological differ-ences in strength cannot yet be estimated.(15)

The work of Wilmore has been particularly important in demonstrating that women's lack of strength in the upper body comes at least in part from disuse rather than totally from biology.(16) In several studies in which nonathletic women and men were tested during training with weights, women's strength was found to increase faster than men's, and women's greatest gains were made in the muscles of the upper body. This much greater relative improvement in women's arm and shoulder strength was attributed to the fact that in daily life, American women already use their lower bodies in ways similar to men, but make much less use of the upper body. Results similar to those of Wilmore have been found during training programs for women cadets at West Point.(17) Furthermore, when we look at differences between individuals in our society, we find that women who use their arms and shoulders a good deal in their work are significantly stronger than average.(18) In some other other societies, "women's work" regularly includes carrying heavy loads or hauling water. It would be interesting to see whether sex differences in upper body strength are much the same as sex differences in leg strength in these societies.

Increased use and development of muscles does not mean that women will necessarily develop the same type of musculature as men. Although strength increases, women in general do not develop the bulging muscles usually associated with men. Typically, women can increase their strength by 50 to 75% without any increase in muscle bulk. This difference in responses to training is probably due to sex differences in levels of testosterone, which seems to be involved in the development of large muscle mass.

The relationship between muscle mass, exercise, and strength is unknown at present. What is clear is that women need not have muscles as large as men in order to be equally strong.(19) The recent research on women is not the only indication of this. It has been known for a long time that lighter male athletes possess proportionally greater muscle power than heavier ones. Wilmore and others have postulated, on the basis of their work with women, that women may have the same potential for strength as men of comparable size even though muscular development is different.

Changes in strength are not the only ones that occur when women become more active physically. Although an average difference in percentage and distribution of body fat persists, women lose relatively more fat during training than men do.(20) (Estrogens and body fat mutually affect each other, but the relationship is complex, with levels of estrogen affecting amounts and distribution of body fat, and body fat, in turn, affecting estrogen levels.) There are clear differences between women athletes and the general population of women. The percentage of body fat, on the average, is lower for the athletes and similar to that for nonathletic men. Some female long distance runners show values as low as 6 or 7%. Sex differences in other physiological measures, such as oxygen uptake or energy utilization, also show a decrease during physical training for women.(21) Changes in sex differences in heat adaptation and sweating are not well established, but since it is well known that adaptation to heat improves with training, it has been suggested that as girls become more active and sweat more when they are young, this sex difference may also decrease.(22)

Somewhat more speculative is the possible effect of exercise on bone growth. Bones are known to become stronger when used. In right-handed women, for example, the bones of the right hand are denser and more substantial than those of the left. Calcium is metabolized best when the muscles that surround the bone are being used, thus stimulating the blood flow to the area. The pull of the muscles on bone may also have an effect. It is possible that similar activity patterns in girls and boys might result in a smaller sex difference in bone formation. There has been speculation that heavy training, particularly prior to puberty, might influence the structural development of the female pelvis(23) — a possibility that some people view with alarm.

There may also be some effects on height, a possibility I will discuss later.

Changes in athletic records show the same trends toward equalization. The number of women athletes has increased significantly in the last few decades, and training programs for women have been taken more seriously, although often only after legal challenges to high school and university sports programs under Title VII of the Civil Rights Act. During this time, women's records have been increasing faster than men's in many athletic events. The greatest relative gains have come in swimming where almost all the top women competitors routinely break men's records of the recent past. In long distance running, the female/male gap has also decreased substantially.

In general, the physical performance of American women athletes differs from that of the average population of nonathletic women much more than that of men athletes does from nonathletic men.(24) Furthermore, women athletes are somewhat closer in physical attributes to men athletes than the average woman is to the average man.

Cross-cultural studies also illustrate that physical development is under a great deal of cultural control, offering further proof that the origins of sex differences in musculature are not simple. In most contemporary societies there is a tendency for men to perform the activities that require a great deal of exertion. Balinese society is an exception, since in the traditional society neither women nor men do much heavy work, with the result that both are slender and show minimal differences in body build. European visitors have complained that they can not tell the women and men apart, even from the front. However, when Balinese men are hired to work on the docks loading ships for Europeans, they develop the heavy musculature we consider typical of males.(25) There are other examples, as well, of societies where sex differences in body type appear to be much smaller than in our culture.

HEIGHT AND ENVIRONMENTAL FACTORS

Height is another anatomical feature that is affected by culture in complex ways that illustrate the difficulties of separating nature and nurture. While height appears to have considerable hereditary components, average height can change substantially for genetically similar populations reared in different environments.(26) Immigrant families to the United States show dramatic increases in height from one generation to the next. Furthermore, although sex differences in average height appear to exist in all cultures, the magnitude can vary considerably. Differences ranging from less than two inches to more than eight have been observed,(27) and within a given society, sex differences in height may change with time. For example, over the last 80 years in Japan the difference has decreased by more than half an inch.(28)

A number of factors other than heredity have been shown to influence height. There is clear evidence of a direct effect of changes in diet on height.(29) Other factors have been pointed to as well: incidence of diseases, amount of sunshine, physical and emotional stress, and amount of physical activity.

Diet is often given as the sole cause of changes in the height of immigrants to the United States. However, changes in diet are often accompanied by other changes which may also affect height. Much of the evidence linking diet with stature is based on the positive correlation between height and socioeconomic class, but clearly, many differences other than diet distinguish classes. Hard physical labor and increased incidence of diseases, as well as a bad diet, are often the lot of those at the bottom of the social hierarchy. Infant care practices that differ by class may also affect growth. Thus, class differences in stature, which are well documented in nineteenth century Britain and in a number of other countries, are probably due to a number of circumstances, of which diet is only one.

In one study, two anthropologists have used cross-cultural data to try to assess the effect of physical stress in infancy.(30) They examined effects on average male height of stressful infant rearing practices, such as customs that involved either piercing or molding some part of the body. Average adult male height was found to be over two inches greater in the stressed groups. The usual variables thought to affect height – genetic factors and diet – were controlled for in this work. Thus, the difference would appear to be primarily due to cultural variables. It could be due to differences in stress or to some other cultural variables that correlate with this particular type of treatment. Corroborating such a cultural interpretation is another study cited by these authors (though on a very small sample), in which it was found that handling premature infants was correlated with accelerated growth.

Cultural effects on height are probably mediated by hormones, for various hormones affect height, including pituitary growth hormone and some sex hormones, and the levels of these hormones are influenced by a variety of cultural factors, including stress and exercise.(31) For example, the levels of growth hormone seem to respond to even minor changes in the environment. In normal individuals, levels of growth hormone vary in relation to food intake and activity, and there is a significant response to exercise. However, the degree to which growth is affected by the normal variations in hormone levels that result from different environments and behaviors is largely unknown. Some studies have claimed that psychologically stressful situations not only can inhibit growth hormone secretion in children, but that this can be sufficient to affect growth.(32) For example, one study showed that children who suffered severe emotional deprivation in their home-life were severely retarded in their growth and had abnormal growth hormone responses. When they were removed to new and better environments, they began to grow rapidly.(33)

Differences in upbringing, then, may affect growth for a variety of reasons, and it is possible that these differences influence sex differences in height. There are many ways in which girls and boys are treated differently, and some of the height differences between the sexes may be a reflection of early environmental differences.

Sex differences in height also could be due in part to the consistent sex differences that exist between girls and boys in activity and in the kind of sports and play that are encouraged. A long-term growth study on competitive young female swimmers has shown that their growth, as a group, was accelerated above established norms, and that the acceleration was greater during their training years.(34)

Correlations between activity levels and height may be attributable to a number of hormonal effects. As we have seen, activity may directly affect growth hormone production. It may also affect "sex hormone" levels, which, in turn, can affect height. The production of estrogens by females at puberty, for example, retards long bone growth, thus leading on the average to smaller females. But since estrogen levels vary with activity, final adult height may be affected by physical activity during adolescence. Estrogen levels are also affected by the degree of body fat, which is itself indirectly affected by activity levels.

In some cultures, not only average height but also sex differences in height may be influenced by diet. Among peoples where dietary deficiencies are affecting height, the effects may be different for women and men, since in marginal situations boys sometimes get a more adequate diet than girls do. There is also the possibility that even where the diet is adequate nutritionally, differences in diet may cause differences in height, and in many societies there is a significant difference in the foods eaten by girls and boys.

I do not mean to suggest that if females and males were raised in the same way there would be no average difference in strength or height. At this point we have no way of knowing what would happen under these circumstances. However, the variation in sex differences in height cross-culturally, historically, and currently in different social classes indicates that these differences, just as with strength, are at least in part the results of environmental factors. How significant these factors are or how they might change from one environment to another remains to be established.

INTELLECTUAL ABILITIES AND THE BRAIN

The different social roles of women and men are often said to be due to sex differences in mental capacities. In fact, the notion that inherited mental abilities are a major factor in determining social position has been one of the most tenacious ideas of the last 100 years. People – usually those in positions of privilege – have, for example, repeatedly ascribed the disadvantaged positions of women relative to men or of Blacks relative to whites to differences in intellectual abilities or traits. Widespread assumptions of innate sex, class, and ethnic differences in mental characteristics have had a major influence on efforts to measure mental abilities and have encouraged attempts to find a biological basis for differences in these abilities. At times scientists have concentrated on trying to show that differences in abilities exist between different groups. At other times, they have been more interested in finding some measurable physical differences in the brains of different groups which might give rise to differences in mental performance. The effect of the underlying assumptions is clear in both cases. Either way, scientists attempt to find tools to measure the differences that are <u>assumed</u> to be there, rather than to examine whether or not the differences actually exist. Results that do not come out as expected are blamed on faulty methodology or bad data and rejected. Since the criteria for acceptability of a given test of mental abilities (such as the IQ test) are usually not based on a particular theory of intelligence (since none exists) but rather on the test's ability to provide expected results, it is often not at all clear what is being measured. This means that, even more than for the body characteristics discussed in the previous section, it is often difficult to say what differences in mental characteristics exist between groups. And no one can say what any measured difference might reveal about the way people function in society.(35)

In order to understand the problems of current research in this area, it is helpful to take a brief look at past work. Craniology, the measurement of skull and brain size, was an important scientific field during the nineteenth century when much work was done on mental abilities and the brain.(36) Craniologists assumed that "intelligence" was directly related to brain size and therefore began measuring the sizes of brains, or rather, of skulls. The results at first bore out expectations: whites appeared to have bigger brains than Native Americans, orientals, or Blacks. In fact, the measurements were incorrect, since, on average, there are no racial differences in brain size. The force of the underlying assumptions was simply so great that the expected results were obtained. A recent reexamination of some of the data shows the powerful effect of bias on scientific research, for the misinterpretation of the measurements appears to have been completely unconscious.(37) Needless to say, it was also clear to craniologists that if brain size were correlated with intelligence, men must have bigger brains than women. In this case, no manipulation of data was required to reach the expected result, since on average women do have smaller brains than men. But then it became apparent that body size had to be taken into account, since if sheer brain size were to be the measure of mental capacity, elephants and whales would be the most intelligent creatures. This dilemma turned out to be the downfall of craniology: there was no obvious and generally agreed upon way of handling the measurements so as to come out with proper anatomical reasons for men's assumed intellectual superiority over women. By some measures, such as the ratio of brain surface to body surface, women were inferior intellectually to men, while by others, such as ratio of brain weight to body weight, women came out ahead.

This problem eventually led to the disappearance of craniology as a serious scientific field. It was replaced by IQ testing, which undertook the measurement of mental abilities rather than physical differences.(38) IQ tests were originally developed as a way to predict performance in school. They have since not only come to be seen as measures of intelligence, but intelligence has come to be defined in terms of whatever abilities are measured on an IQ test. For the last 50 years these tests and others derived using similar methods have dominated research on group differences in mental abilities. Until recently, there has been little interest in demonstrating possible underlying biological differences, but we are currently seeing a revival of interest in this question.(39)

Current theories of innate sex differences in mental abilities, unlike their nineteenth century counterparts, usually do not claim that women are less intelligent than men. Instead they focus on sex differences that are observed in tests of different types of mental abilities. This shift in interest is a result of peculiarities in IQ tests. Although they do show class and race differences when total scores are compared, IQ tests do not yield overall sex differences. Instead women do better on certain kinds of questions identified as more verbal, while men do better on questions measuring mathematical and visual-spatial ability.(40) On early tests combining both types of questions, women scored higher than men, which prompted the test designers to include appropriate numbers of each type of question so as to eliminate the sex difference in the overall score.

Recently, the sex differences in verbal and spatial-visual abilities have become the focus of attention, and a number of theories have tried to tie these differences in performance to innate differences in the brains of women and men.

One widely publicized group of theories suggests that the human brain is programmed before birth by sex hormones. These prenatal influences are said to result later in sex differences in these kinds of mental abilities as well as in such traits as aggressiveness and reproductive behavior.(41) This claim is based on studies in which differences can be seen in the patterns of nerve fiber connections in certain regions of the brains of female and male mice – regions that are specifically associated with reproductive behavior. Studies of correlations between hormone levels and mating behavior in laboratory animals are also cited as evidence. Other kinds of studies involve people with various genetic and hormonal abnormalities. The many problems with the data used and their interpretation have been thoroughly discussed by a number of people.(42) The most important problem with the human behavioral studies is that they have failed to control for any effect of environmental differences encountered by people with and without the observed abnormalities.(43)

Another attempt to explain the origin of sex differences in mental abilities is provided by theories suggesting that innate sex differences exist in the way the two halves or hemispheres of the brain are used. In humans, although the interactions of the two sides of the brain are complex, the right and left halves are to some extent specialized for different functions and used to a somewhat different extent depending on the tasks that are being performed.   (This is called lateralization.)(44) The left hemisphere is usually more active during verbal tasks and during tests that involve analytical and linear thought patterns, while the right hemisphere is more active when a person is visualizing or manipulating objects in space or thinking intuitively or associatively. Anatomical differences have been reported between the left and right sides of the human brain, but it has not been established whether these are related to lateralization of function.(45) It is clear that even though there must be some relationship between anatomy and function, lateralization of function cannot be rigidly connected with brain anatomy. For one thing, after lesions to one side of the brain that have resulted in loss of function, such as speech, recovery sometimes occurs by the other side taking over the function.(46) Children usually experience complete recovery, which makes it appear likely that the two halves of the brain initially are equipotential, or nearly so, and specialize only after the first few years of life. Studies of brain electrical activity also provide evidence that brain lateralization can be affected by environment and behavior, and that it is by no means a fixed or "wired-in" aspect of brain functioning.(47) What these studies show is that the type and degree of asymmetry appears to be affected by mood, motivation, and training. For example, after biofeedback training, people are able to produce more or less asymmetry at will on tasks for which they preferentially used one or the other side of the brain before the training.

Numerous investigators have claimed that they can demonstrate a connection between sex differences in brain lateralization and sex differences in verbal and spatial abilities, but such claims are largely fact-free speculation.(48) In spite of large numbers of studies,(49) there is no good, clear-cut evidence for sex differences in brain lateralization. Several different types of evidence have been offered. There are studies that indicate sex differences on various tasks designed to probe brain lateralization.(50) However, the results have been inconsistent enough to make the existence of such differences highly uncertain. Furthermore, even if differences in performance do exist, the relationship to differences in brain lateralization is not clear. A number of difficulties in interpretation have been pointed out. For example, some studies have involved auditory tasks, and possible sex differences in hearing thresholds may exist. A general difficulty is that differences in performance could be due to sex differences in strategies used to solve problems rather than differences in brain functioning.(51) Clinical observations have been another source of data on sex differences in performance. For example, observations that verbal skills of females are less disrupted by damage to the left hemisphere than those of males have been taken as an indication of sex differences in lateralization, but this interpretation has been severely criticized.(52) Studies of electrical activity of the brain show some kinds of sex differences in hemispheric asymmetry during the performance of particular tasks, but these differences are complex and seem again to be affected by personality and behavioral factors, such as motivation, practice, or strategies chosen to perform the task. The differences are also changed with biofeedback training.(53)

Given the ambiguous evidence, it is likely that investigators who propose theories connecting sex differences in mental abilities with brain lateralization simply couple the fact that there are sex differences in performance on spatial and verbal tasks with the observation that the brain is lateralized for these functions. They assume from this that some sex differences in lateralization must exist and set about looking for them, often using as measures the very behavioral differences they are trying to explain. The lack of any real foundation for this work can be seen by the fact that the two principal theories have arrived at opposite assumptions as to what the sex differences in brain lateralization might be.(54) One of these theories is more widely accepted than the other at present, but both are still seen as possible. Both theories can persist simultaneously only because there is no real evidence to support either one.

There is a general difficulty with trying to make a straightforward connection between sex differences in brain lateralization and sex differences in behavior. The way skills are assumed to be divided up between the two halves of the brain is not the same way skills are divided up between women and men. The left half of the brain is believed to be more specialized for verbal, analytical, and logical skills, but women do better on verbal tests and men are widely held to be more analytical and logical. The right half of the brain, on the other hand, appears to be more involved in spatial visual ability, at which men are better, and in intuitive thinking, a trait usually assigned to women. Explanations that try to fit brain lateralization to sex stereotypes necessarily end up with some major contortions.

Work on brain lateralization illustrates some of the difficulties in trying to find causal relationships between anatomy, physiology, and brain function. Even if sex differences in brain lateralization were to be demonstrated more clearly than is at present the case, and if some correlation were to be established with sex differences in verbal and spatial skills, we would still have no information on the origins of the differences. Given the evidence that experience and training affect brain lateralization, it is perfectly possible that differential socialization and learning can lead to differences in brain lateralization, instead of or in addition to differences arising from innate factors. Some work has suggested, for example, that since girls seem to acquire verbal skills earlier than boys, they may be predisposed to develop verbal strategies, and that this may be evidence for sex differences in brain lateralization. This early acquisition of verbal ability could come from some innate biological difference, perhaps related to lateralization. It could come from the fact that parents, teachers, and others talk differently to little girls and boys, which might lead to differences in lateralization, or it could come from a combination of the two. At present, however, there is no way of separating the effects of these two factors, of knowing their relationship to brain lateralization, or even of knowing whether they are the right ones to consider.

Any theories postulating that innate differences in the brain lead to behavioral differences involve the same difficulties as the brain lateralization or sex hormone theories. The relationship among anatomy, physiology, and behavioral functions is not at all clear, nor is the extent to which all of these are influenced by the environment. We do, however, have a number of research findings indicating that environmental effects on the human brain cannot be neglected.(55) Though none of the work on the brain is definitive, it illustrates the problem inherent in all attempts to attribute human behavioral differences to innate differences in brain structure or function: there is no way to eliminate the possibility that brain differences may have resulted from behavioral or environmental differences rather than the other way around.

SEX HORMONES

Work on sex hormones is another politically loaded area, since interpretations of results often end up reinforcing sex role stereotypes. It has been widely assumed that average differences in sex hormones must contribute to average differences in behavior. In an effort to prove this, scientists have tried to show that variations in hormone levels within each sex are tied to variations in behavior. One of the primary difficulties with these attempts is that hormone levels themselves are affected by behavior and environment, so that no causal relationships can be established. For example, it is claimed that levels of the so-called male hormone, testosterone, determine aggression and social ranking both among male nonhuman primates and people.(56) The case of testosterone and social ranking in nonhuman primates provides a classic example of how wrong it is to make assumptions about causes when only correlations are being observed. Although hormone levels do indeed correlate with rank in dominance hierarchies among male rhesus monkeys, for example, studies indicate that hormone levels do not determine position in the hierarchies.(57) When the social rank of individuals changes, their hormonal activity also changes. It is not clear whether the experience of dominance increases testosterone production or whether being in a subordinate position decreases it, or both. In general, it is found that psychological, physical, or social stress can lower both social rank and testosterone levels.

In humans, no correlations have been found between levels of testosterone and social rank or aggression. However, social environment, exercise, psychological states and physical stress all affect testosterone levels.(58)

Another difficulty arises with trying to connect hormones and behavior. There is evidence that the relationship between hormonal states and behavioral and emotional states varies in different situations. For the same person, the same hormonal state can be associated with a number of different behaviors, depending on the social setting. For example, one experiment indicated that if the adrenal system is aroused through injections of adrenal hormones in a situation where anger is an appropriate response, then the response comes out as anger. If euphoria is a more appropriate response to a given situation, then people become euphoric.(59)

Hormonal contributions to behavior, then, depend in part on the levels of hormones at a particular moment, which are themselves determined by a person's past interactions with the social environment and in part on the details of the curent social environment. It is not possible to abstract behavior from its social context.

WHAT IS THE POINT OF ALL THIS?

Biological determinism is a particular way of viewing causes of social structures. It offers a specific, scientifically-based model for the existence of social hierarchy and social inequality by postulating that differences in innate biology lead to differences in behavior, which in turn lead to differences in social position.

In the previous sections we have seen some of the flaws in the scientific basis of the biological determinist model: that biology cannot be taken as something fixed and immutable, and that it is generally not possible to show that a given biological state causes a specific behavior. Biology does affect human behavior, but the examples I have discussed make it clear that there is no way to separate the contributions biology and culture make to behavioral differences.

It is the second step in the biological determinist model that is of political importance, since this step gives the model its specific political character. It is the desire to explain observed social differences that leads biological determinists to look at differences between the sexes, races, or classes. The implications for social change are what impel others to listen to what biological determinists have to say. However, this model is no better at establishing the connection between behavior and social position than it is at showing the connection between a genetically programmed biology and behavior.

Biological determinists often argue that it is primarily ability or talent, independent of sex or race, that determines social position in our society. This assertion is contradicted by a number of studies of social opportunity and mobility in the United States.(60) Furthermore, if we look specifically at sex differences, we find immediate evidence to refute this claim. Women and men are, in general, much more alike than different, and the magnitude of observed average differences in behavior or abilities (which may in fact be overestimated) is much smaller than are the differences between women's and men's social roles. For example, differences in mathematical ability are often cited as the reason for the small number of women scientists and engineers. But the differences in participation rates of women and men in scientific fields in our society are so much larger than the reported sex differences in mathematical ability that differences in ability could not begin to account for the different numbers of women and men scientists.(61) In general, observed sex and race differences in behavior would explain only a small part of our social hierarchy, even if merit and ability were the most important factors.

Another version of "biology is destiny" suggests that women's nature is such that only certain social roles are appropriate. Since the nineteenth century, it has been widely held that woman's work needs to be more closely scrutinized, regulated, and restricted because of her special role as reproducer and rearer of children. The inconsistencies that are discovered when the restrictions are examined, however, suggest that the aim is more to maintain a sexually segregated labor force than to protect future generations. Women are excluded from certain hazardous jobs, but not from others. In general, the exclusion is from the higher paying, male dominated jobs and not from equally hazardous ones that have traditionally been seen as women's work.

It is apparent that the importance attached to biological explanations of sex, race, or class differences in ability, behavior, or social role comes from the political content of the theories rather than from their scientific merit. If race and sex and class were not politically and economically significant categories, it is likely that no one would care very much about biological differences between members of these groups. To pay attention to the study of sex differences would be rather peculiar in a society where their political importance was small. Biological determinist theories, which pretend to explain why the world is the way it is, are built on the myth that social structures are determined by the biological nature of human beings. As we have seen, the political messages are usually quite explicit. The theories would have us believe that the only way women and men or Blacks and whites could have equal social positions would be if opportunities were rigged to compensate for intrinsic deficiencies.

The proponents of these theories often accuse their critics of reading too much into their ideas. They emphasize that difference does not necessarily imply inequality. But what they ignore is the reality of our society, where social inequality has been constructed along biological lines and indeed even contributes to biological differences.

Biodeterminist theories have reappeared at this particular time because we are in a period of major social change, the eventual outcome of which is uncertain. The movement of women into the wage labor force during the last decades has resulted in important changes in the lives of everyone. Meanwhile, the appearance of the women's movement has encouraged the explicit discussion of issues raised by these changes and has helped to raise women's expectations for equal rights and opportunities. However, these increased expectations pose a threat to the maintenance of many existing social structures. Therefore, it is not surprising that we now see women's demands for equal opportunity being met by arguments about biological limitations. The current theories about the biological basis of social structures − the theories that say, for example, that women are "naturally" disadvantaged – are of use to those who want to preserve and strengthen the dominant political and economic interests. One result is that a great deal of media attention is given to biological theories that offer naturalistic explanations for the distribution of wealth and power in this society.

Since these theories are so persuasive and politically loaded, we cannot ignore them or allow them to go unchallenged. But we must be clear about why feminists should examine the question of the possible existence of biologically-based sex differences. We should do so only in response to the claims of biological determinists who say that these differences have social significance and that a knowledge of them provides a guide to social policy and to the limits of possible social change. We should not try to make a knowledge of the origins of sex differences the basis of our own vision of the future. Indeed, we could not even if we wanted to. Contrary to the claims of biological determinists, studies of the contributions that biological factors make to human behavior can at most give only very limited information about the origins of present differences in human behavior and probably no information about the origins of present social structures. Such studies offer no insight into the effects of social change on behavior. Whatever sex differences in behavior exist now and whatever their origins, we have no reason to assume that they would be barriers to any egalitarian society we may want to build.

NOTES

(1) See for example: Edward O. Wilson, Sociobiology, The New Synthesis (Cambridge, Mass.: Harvard University Press, 1975); Alice S. Rossi, "The Biosocial Side of Parenthood," Human Nature 1 (June 1978): 72-79.

(2) See Marian Lowe and Ruth Hubbard, "Sociobiology and Bio-sociology," in Ruth Hubbard and Marian Lowe, eds., Genes and Gender II: Pitfalls in Research on Sex and Gender (New York: Gordian Press, 1979), pp. 91-111 and references therein.

(3) J.W. Berry, "Tenine and Eskimo Perceptual Skills," International Journal of Psychology 1 (1966): 207-229; A.G. Goldstein and J.E. Chance, "Effects of Practice on Sex-related Differences in Performance on Embedded Figures," Psychomonic Science 3 (1965): 361-362; Janet M. Conner, Lisa A. Serbin and Maxine Schackman, "Sex Differences in Children's Response to Training on a Visual-Spatial Test," Developmental Psychology 13 (1977): 293-294; Beatrice Whiting and Carolyn Pope Edwards, "A Cross-Cultural Analysis of Sex Differences in the Behavior of Children Age 3-11," Journal of Social Psychology 91 (1973): 171-188; Katherine F. Bradway and Clare W. Thompson, "Intelligence at Adulthood: A 25-Year Followup," Journal of Educational Psychology 53 (1962): 1-14.

(4) This is one of the factors in the resistance to the participation of women in athletics. It becomes harder to maintain our cultural stereotypes of female fragility and passivity when women play contact sports, run fifty miles, or lead Himalayan expeditions.

(5) The acceptance of the inevitable superiority of male strength on the part of both women and men also contributes to men's violence against women and may in part explain women's hesitation to resist.

(6) Eleanor E. Maccoby and Carol N. Jacklin, The Psychology of Sex Differences (Stanford, Calif.: Stanford University Press, 1974), pp. 307-311.

(7) Statistical Abstracts of the United States (U.S. Department of Commerce, 1978), p. 121.

(8) Robert M. Malina, "Quantification of Fat, Muscle and Bone in Man," Clinical Orthopaedics 65 (1969): 9-38; Donald K. Mathews and Edward L. Fox, The Physiological Basis of Physical Education and Athletics, 2nd ed. (Philadelphia: W.B. Saunders Co., 1976).

(9) B. Lofstedt, Human Heat Tolerance (Lund: Department of Hygiene, University of Lund, Sweden, 1966).

(10) Donald K. Mathews and Edward L. Fox, Physiological Basis, pp. 452-460.

(11) In measures of performance, effects of expectations by both experimenters and students may not be negligible. The actual strength of women, particularly in the United States, may have been underestimated for this reason. For women the social stigma attached to being strong may well affect our actual performance on strength tests. Women have been conditioned throughout our lives not to appear strong, and we may not ignore these social expectations, particularly when the test is administered by a male, as is usually the case.

(12) Donald K. Mathews and Edward L. Fox, Physiological Basis, pp. 460-466.

(13) Ibid., pp. 447-450; John H. Douglas and Julie Ann Miller, "Record Breaking Women," Science News 112 (1977): 172-174; Ellen W. Gerber et al. The American Woman in Sport (Reading, Mass.: Addison-Wesley, 1974), pp. 403-418; Joan Ullyot, Women's Running (Mountain View, Calif.: World Publications, 1976), p. 91. It should not surprise us that most money-making professional sports emphasize areas where men have the advantage. Football depends on physical size and strength. Among sports, it is the epitome of male brute strength. Basketball depends on height, baseball on upper arm strength and speed, and hockey on willingness to use physical violence. For a further discussion

of the role of sports in maintaining cultural stereotypes, see Michael Albert and Robin Hahnel, Unorthodox Marxism (Boston: South End Press, 1978), pp. 218-220.

(14) Joan Ullyot, Women's Running, p. 96.

(15) John H. Douglas and Julie Ann Miller, "Record Breaking Women," p. 172.

(16) Jack H. Wilmore, "Alterations in Strength, Body Composition and Anthropometric Measurements Consequent to a 10-Week Weight Training Program," Medicine and Science in Sports 6 (1974): 133-138; Jack H. Wilmore, "Inferiority of Female Athletes, Myth or Reality," Journal of Sports Medicine 3 (1975): 1-6.

(17) J. Peterson and D. Kowal, Project 60: A Comparison of Two Types of Physical Training Programs on the Performance of 16-18 Year Old Women (West Point: Office of Physical Education, 1977).

(18) Miriam G. Wardle and David S. Gloss, "Women's Capacity to Perform Strenuous Work," Women and Health 5 (1980): 5-15.

(19) Ernst Jokl, Physiology of Exercise (Springfield, Illinois: Charles C. Thomas, 1964), p. 64.

(20) Jack H. Wilmore, "Body Composition and Strength Development," Journal of Physical Education and Recreation 46 (1975): 38-40; C. Harmon Brown and Jack H. Wilmore, "The Effects of Maximal Resistance Training on the Strength and Body Composition of Women Athletes," Medicine and Science in Sports 6 (1974): 174-177.

(21) Ellen W. Gerber et al., The American Woman in Sport, pp. 455-485.

(22) Dorothy Harris, "Survival of the Sweatiest," Women's Sports (November, 1977); B.L. Drinkwater and S.M. Horvath, "Heat Tolerance and Aging." Medicine and Science in Sports 11 (1979): 49-55

(23) J. Kaplan, Woman and Sport (New York, Viking, 1979), p. 40; Ellen Gerber et al., The American Woman in Sport, p. 440.

(24) Ellen W. Gerber et al., The American Woman in Sport, p. 421.

(25) Geoffrey Gorer, Bali and Angkor (London: Michael Joseph, 1936).

(26) J.M. Tanner, "Growing Up," Scientific American 229 (September 1973): 35-43.

(27) Ann Oakley, Sex, Gender and Society (New York: Harper Colophon, 1972), p. 28.

(28) S. Suzuki et al., "Interrelationships between Nutrition, Physical Activity and Physical Fitness," in Jana Parizkova and V.A. Rogozkin, eds., Nutrition, Physical Fitness and Health (Baltimore: University Park Press, 1978).

(29) Rose E. Frisch, "Population, Food Intake and Fertility," Science 199 (1978): 22-30.

(30) T. Landauer and J. Whiting, "Infantile Stimulation and Adult Stature of Human Males," in Victor H. Denenberg, ed., The Development of Behavior (Stamford: Sinauer Associates, 1972).

(31) K. Kuoppasalmi et al., "Effect of Strenuous Anaerobic Running Exercise on Plasma Growth Hormone, Cortisol, Luteinizing Hormone, Testosterone, Androstenedione, Estrone and Estradiol," Journal of Steroid Biochemistry 7 (1976): 823-829; Janet Jurkowski et al., "Ovarian Hormonal Responses to Exercise," Journal of Applied Psychology 44 (1978): 109-114; L. Levi, "Sympatho-adrenomedullary and Related Biochemical Reactions During Experimentally Induced Emotional Stress," in Richard P. Michael, ed., Endocrinology and Human Behavior (New York: Oxford University Press, 1968); Seymour Reichlin, "Hypothalamic Control of Growth Hormone Secretion and the Response to Stress," Ibid., pp. 256-283.

(32) Lytt I. Gardner, "Deprivation Dwarfism," Scientific American 227 (July 1972): 76-83.

(33) Elinor D. Powell et al., "Growth Hormone in Relation to Diabetic Retinopathy," New England Journal of Medicine 275 (1966): pp. 922-925. It is important to be cautious in interpreting this kind of work. Children in "emotionally deprived" homes also may have been nutritionally deprived, either because they did not get sufficient food or because they were too upset to eat. Thus, even though hormonal abnormalities were noted, one cannot easily assign causes.

(34) G. Lawrence Rareck, "Exercise and Growth," in Warren R. Johnson and E.R. Buskirk, eds., Science and the Medicine of Exercise and Sport (New York: Harper & Row, 1973). This study needs to be interpreted with care, as do all studies comparing athletes to the general population. It is possible that there is a self-selection process, by which girls with certain kinds of physical characteristics are more likely to be found training as athletes. Such caution is especially indicated when looking at changes in age of onset of menstruation. It may be that late onset means, for girls, a postponement of the social pressures associated with puberty and thus more freedom to continue with athletics in a serious way.

(35) Even in measuring physical differences, experimenter bias can distort observed characteristics.

(36) Elizabeth Fee, "Nineteenth Century Craniology: The Study of the Female Skull," Bulletin of the History of Medicine 53 (1979): 415-433.

(37) Stephen J. Gould, "Morton's Ranking of Races by Cranial Capacity," Science 200 (1978): 503-509.

(38) Robert A. McCall, Intelligence and Heredity (Homewood, Illinois: Learning Systems Company, 1975).

(39) Ashton Barfield, "Biological Influences on Sex Differences in Behavior," in Michael S. Teitelbaum, ed., Sex Differences: Social and Biological Perspectives (Garden City, N.Y.: Anchor Books, 1976).

(40) Eleanor Maccoby and Carol Jacklin, Psychology of Sex Differences, pp. 349-360.

(41) John Money and Anke A. Ehrhardt, Man and Woman, Boy and Girl (Baltimore: Johns Hopkins Press, 1972); Alice S. Rossi, "A Biological Perspective on Parenting," Daedalus 106 (1977): 1031; Donald M. Broverman, Edward L. Klaiber and William Bogel, "Gonadal Hormones and Cognitive Functioning," in Jacquelynne E. Parsons, ed., The Psychology of Sex Differences and Sex Roles (New York: McGraw Hill, 1980).

(42) Estelle Ramey, "Sex Hormones and Executive Ability," Annals of the New York Academy of Sciences 208 (1973): 237-245; also see the articles by Freda Salzman, Ruth Bleier, and Marian Lowe and Ruth Hubbard, in Ruth Hubbard and Marian Lowe, eds., Genes and Gender II.

(43) Barbara Fried, "Boys Will Be Boys Will Be Boys," in Ruth Hubbard, Mary Sue Henifin, and Barbara Fried, eds., Biological Woman - The Convenient Myth (Cambridge, Mass.: Schenkman, 1982), pp. 47-69.

(44) Jerre Levy-Agresti and Roger Sperry, "Differential Perceptual Capacities in Major and Minor Hemispheres," Proceedings of the National Academy of Sciences 61 (1968): 1151-1162; Roger W. Sperry, "Lateral Specialization in the Surgically Separated Hemispheres," in Francis O. Schmitt and Frederic G. Wordon, eds., The Neurosciences: Third Study Program (Cambridge, Mass.: M.I.T. Press, 1974).

(45) Norman Geschwind, "The Anatomical Basis of Hemispheric Differentiation," in Stuart J. Dimond and J. Graham Beaumont, eds., Hemisphere Function in the Human Brain (New York: Wiley, 1974).

(46) H. Hecaen, "Acquired Aphasia in Children," Brain and Language 3 (1976): 114-134.

(47) Richard J. Davidson and Gary E. Schwartz, "Patterns of Cerebral Lateralization during Cardiac Biofeedback versus the Self-regulation of

Emotion; Sex Differences," Psychophysiology 13 (1976): 62-68; Y. Matsumiya, "The Psychological Significance of Stimuli and Cerebral Evoked Response Asymmetry," in David I. Mostofsky, Behavior Control and Modification of Physiological Activity (Englewood Cliffs, N.J.: Prentice Hall, 1976).

(48) Susan Leigh Star, "Sex Differences and the Dichotomization of the Brain," in Ruth Hubbard and Marian Lowe, eds., Genes and Gender II.

(49) Jeannette McGlone, "Sex Differences in Human Brain Asymmetry: A Critical Survey," Behavioral and Brain Sciences 3 (1980): 215-263.

(50) Deborah P. Waber, "Sex Differences in Mental Abilities, Hemispheric Lateralization and Rate of Physical Growth at Adolescence," Developmental Psychology 13 (1977): 29-38; Sandra F. Witelson, "Sex and the Single Hemisphere: Specialization of the Right Hemisphere for Spatial Processing," Science 193 (1976): 425-427; J. Bradshaw and A. Gates, "Visual Field Differences in Verbal Tasks: Effects of Task Familiarity and Sex of Subject," Brain and Language 5 (1978): 166-187.

(51) M. Bryden, "Strategy Effects in the Assessment of Hemispheric asymmetry," in G. Underwood, ed., Strategies of Information Processing (New York: Academic, 1978): pp. 117-149.

(52) J. Bogan, "The Other Side of the Brain II: An Appositional Mind," Bulletin of the Los Angeles Neurological Societies 34 (1969): 135-162; H. Lansdell, "A Sex Difference in Effect of Temporal-Lobe Neuro-surgery on Design Preference," Nature 194 (1962): 852-854; McClone, "Sex Differences," pp. 215-217, 227-250.

(53) Y. Matsumiya, "The Psychological Significance of Stimuli."

(54) W. Buffery and J. Gray, "Sex Differences in the Development of Spatial and Linguistic Skill," in C. Ounsted and D. Taylor, eds., Gender Differences: Their Ontogeny and Significance (Edinburgh: Churchill Livingstone, 1972); Jerre Levy, "Lateral Specialization of the Human Brain: Behavioral Manifestations and Possible Evolutionary Basis," in John A. Kiger, The Biology of Behavior (Corvallis, Oregon: Oregon State University Press, 1972).

(55) See, for example, Steven Rose, The Conscious Brain (New York: Random House, 1976).

(56) Eleanor E. Maccoby and Carol Jacklin, Psychology of Sex Differences, p. 243, 368; Steven Goldberg, The Inevitability of Patriarchy (New York: Morrow, 1973).

(57) Arthur Kling, "Testosterone and Aggressive Behavior in Man and Non-human Primates," in Basil Eleftheriou and Richard L. Sprott, eds., Hormonal Correlates of Behavior (New York: Plenum Press, 1975).

(58) C.J. Hale, "Physiological Maturity of Little League Baseball Players," Research Quarterly 27 (1956): 276-284; L.E. Kreuz, R.A. Rose and J.R. Jennings, "Suppression of Plasma Testosterone Levels and Physiological Stress," Archives of General Psychiatry 26 (1972): 479-482; K. Kuoppasalmi et al., "Effects of Strenuous Anaerobic Running Exercise on Plasma Growth Hormone, Cortisol, Luteinizing Hormone, Testosterone, Androstendione, Estrone, and Estradiol," Journal of Steroid Biochemistry 7 (1976): 823-829.

(59) Stanley Schachter and Jerome B. Singer, "Cognitive, Social and Psychological Determinants of Emotional State," Psychological Review 69 (1969): 379-399.

(60) Christopher Jencks, Who Gets Ahead: The Determinants of Economic Success in America (New York: Basic Books, 1979); Peter M. Blau and Otis Dudley Duncan, American Occupational Structure (Riverside, N.J.: Macmillan, 1978); Richard H. de Lone, Small Futures: Children, Inequality and the Limits of Liberal Reform (New York: Harcourt Brace, Jovanovich, 1979).

(61) Meredith M. Kimball, "A Critique of Biological Theories of Sex Differences," International Journal of Women's Studies 4 (1981): 318-333.

occurrence is constantly invoked by most Lakota people — male and female — as indicating the high esteem in which women are held in the culture. There have been many interpretations of this mythological character. Hassrick succinctly gives the following analysis as validating the subjugation of women and as justification for the "double standard."

> The Oedipean nature of the White Buffalo Maiden legend may owe part of its origin to the masculine character of the society. The role of the two scouts, one representing greed and lust and the other respect and temperance, typifies the dual nature of the Sioux character. The White Buffalo Maiden symbolized not only the mother but more significantly, the sister, and she characterized herself as such. In her was embodied the female kin toward whom males must sublimate the sex drive under penalty of death. Conversely, she became the protector of women against the lust of men. That the sex act carried such strong taboo dramatizes the conflict under which the Sioux male existed, and suggests the origin for the double standard. The need for symbolizing such restrictive association for a related female seems to have found compensation in the attitude that unrelated females were the natural target for male seduction. Such women were fair game. The lustful hunter was destroyed not so much for his uncontrollable lust as for his breach of a taboo and his commission of a sacrilege.
>   That the Sioux chose for their tutelary deity a woman, rather than a man, indicates their concern to revere feminine qualities. That the Buffalo Maiden was, in fact, the Goddess Whope, wife of Okaga, the South Wind, enforced the proposition that the Sioux savior was completely and wholesomely feminine. She firmly established a rigid yet healthy realistic sexual pattern to which both its men and women could subscribe, and which they could respect.(3)

I quote this in full, for seldom in the ethnographic record is such an explicitly masculine interpretation of a mythological narrative found. This interpretation seems to give ideological justification for strong control over women. I note, however, another variation of the myth of the White Buffalo Maiden from a native Lakota male religious practitioner (from the yuwipi cult). Lame Deer indicates:

> The White Buffalo Woman then addressed the women, telling them that it was the work of their hands and the fruit of their wombs which kept the tribe alive. "You are from mother earth," she told them. "The task which has been given you is as great as the one given to the warrior and hunter." And therefore, the sacred pipe is also something which binds men and women in a circle of love.(4)

In a more recent statement, a practicing religious leader, Stanley Looking Horse, further notes:

It is told that the red bowl of the Pipe shall represent the feminine aspect while the tube handle of the Pipe shall represent the male aspect. Thus, inclusion of everyone is intended, and if we honor this commitment, then our people will be able to see a great generation.(5)

Through the use of Siouan symbolic structure, the sexual, social, and economic expectations of female behavior are clearly articulated. The cultural mandates from symbolic and mythic structures did actually reflect duality and complementarity in economic and social roles. The survival and continuity of the group depended upon this functional relationship. This was enacted and validated in such ceremonies as the Sun Dance.

Native evaluations of Lakota womanhood are significant, however. The creative ability of the woman to produce children was seen by the Lakota as a powerful act. The native term for pregnancy, eglushaka, translates into English as "growing strong." The wakan (sacredness or power) of a female's menstrual period could weaken the wakan (power) components of such male things as medicine bundles, war bundles, shields, and other paraphernalia, which belonged to the men in the tipi (dwelling). Thus, at the menarche, an emergent woman was placed in a small shelter outside the tipi. This act of isolation was called ishna ti ("to live alone"). It is still used metaphorically to refer to that "time of the moon." In her menstrual dwelling, she was visited by women who were post-menopausal. The isolation was an opportunity for learning excellence in crafts, such as quilling, and tanning hides. Other womanly knowledge involving sexuality and child care was also dispensed. At this time, according to the Lakota view, a woman embodied power and sacredness exactly as she did in a pregnant state. Some interpretations for the Yurok surround such special times with an aura of pollution.(6)

Further, virgin women embodying the sacred White Buffalo Calf Woman were selected to symbolically chop down the sacred Sun Dance pole in the annual summer ceremony. Older women, mostly post-menopausal, assumed the honorific role of the Sacred Pipe Woman.

At present, when difficulties arise in the Sun Dance they are often attributed to women who attend the Sun Dance at the "time of the moon" without knowing the aspects of their power. Indeed, male religious practitioners often blame any untoward event that occurs at such a ritual upon the presence of menstruating women. These new attitudes are a sign of women's repression, no longer an acknowledgement of feminine power.

Such sacred symbols as the White Buffalo Calf Women often serve as a convenient sign that sexual equality is the normative aspect in contemporary Lakota life. The image of this cultural heroine is used as the epitome of Lakota womanhood. This can furthermore be manipulated into the general cultural values of generosity, fortitude, integrity, and wisdom.

Ella Deloria, a native anthropologist and linguist, writes of the Lakota:

Outsiders seeing women keep to themselves have frequently expressed a snap judgment that they were regarded as inferior to the noble male. The simple fact is that woman had her place and man his; they were not the same and neither inferior nor superior.

The sharing of work also was according to sex. Both had to work hard, for their life made severe demands. But neither expected the other to come and help outside the customary division of duties; each sex thought the other had enough to do. That did not mean, however, that a man disdained to do woman's work when necessary; or a woman, man's. The attitude on division of work was quite normal, however it looked to outsiders. A woman caring for children and doing all the work around the house thought herself no worse off than her husband who was compelled to risk his life continuously, hunting and remaining ever on guard against enemy attacks on his family.(7)

Native viewpoints and oral history accounts seem to corroborate Ella Deloria's contentions. With the destruction of the native way of life and the restriction to reservations, disequilibrium was inititated and increased as new belief systems were instigated and forced upon this group of Indians, as they were upon others. Leacock mentions the effects of Christianity upon an Algonkian group in Canada, indicating that a male superiority complex may have been part of an acculturation process.(8) Certainly, the imposition of patrilineality upon many American Indian groups resulted in the use of the father's surname. Hamamsy notes a change in the matrilineal Navajo social structure as a result of superimposed policies.(9) Mary Shepardson's presentation of Irene Stewart's own story adds much to a native perspective of social change in one Navajo woman's life.(10)

There is a drastic need to re-examine the cultural contours of ongoing belief systems in Native North American societies to juxtapose traditional and superimposed ideology and sex role behaviors.

Though attitudes of male superiority are evident in the social organization structures of modern societies, bilaterality was characteristic of the Siouan society in the past. How the change toward patrilineal descent was impressed upon the Lakota and other Plains societies must be examined to assess its contribution to the observable increased masculine bias.

With the prohibition of the Sun Dance as a heathen ritual in the 1800s, a patriarchal male god who condoned punishment for sin did much to disrupt social and economic equity between the sexes. In the early reservation period, the pressure to assimilate all Indians persisted. The treatment of all Lakota males as enemies who were conquered demolished male roles as warriors and hunters. The roles of women as household provisioners and as carers and rearers of children continued. However, under pressure from change agents ("boss farmers" and "matrons" who taught new skills – farming for men and cooking of new foods and sewing of new fabrics for women) there was a disorientation of economic roles and attitudes toward each sex changed. A subtle subordination was imposed on Lakota women. Most did not wish to devalue the demoralized males in the extended families. As survival mechanisms, women became workers in the formal acculturating institutions, such as schools and churches. Some were recruited to go away to school to become teachers or at least matrons in boarding schools. The pressures to accommodate to another and new society were strong. In many cases, an occupational adaptation meant survival for self and kinship units. Much of this adaptation was self-selected with disdain for the native culture. Some alternatives were chosen as a means of rejecting the native society and escaping into a new social world with a new world view and language. Some women simply rejected all aspects of the new society. In any case, coerced cultural change was standard.

There are several possible interpretations of this acculturation process. One is that females who were not "properly trained" in a native cultural system aspired to leave. Another explanation might be that those supporting and committed to the traditional gender ideology remained secure in their kinship networks, economic niche, and natal community. Another segment of females may have compromised and developed a nexus of occupational involvements away from the native group while maintaining a tribal affiliation in kinship bonds, rituals, and aesthetic arenas. Therefore, the ideology and identity tied to tribalness were enacted differently in personal realms.

Development of the above patterns was possible within a changing social order. Clearly, the superimposed ideology of a dominant "American white" culture enforced changes from tribal traditions to a foreign culture. It may be accurately stated that contemporary Lakota Sioux sexism is embedded not only in the biological arena, but in some native ideological structures that have been firmly buttressed by Christian ideology and legal patrilineal codes.

The newly reactivated ritualistic systems, such as the Sun Dance, Wopila ("giving thanks and offerings") and Uwipi ("tying up" the shaman) ceremonies have acknowledged that the foundations for the native belief systems were presented by the White Buffalo Calf Woman. But male orientation in the revitalized native belief structure is strong (as witness, the Lakota Medicine Men's Association which is headquartered at Rosebud reservation, South Dakota). Lakota maidens are still selected to be the four virgins who chose and cut the Sacred Tree; a revered older woman is chosen as the Sacred Pipe Woman. Some women dance in the Sun Dance voluntarily. This is the extent of feminine involvement in this revitalized religious rite. Of course, food preparation and auxiliary features of the ceremony such as the "give-away" rely upon women's work. (A giveaway is a ceremony for the distribution of food, clothing, and other goods in order to make ownership more equitable.) In more traditional areas, however, men still cook the beef. Women, moreover, often carry on the other rites, which are and have been a part of the Sun Dance ritual, such as the "Feeding the Mourners" ceremony, which is still performed at only one Sun Dance among the bands on Standing Rock reservation. These secondary rituals, such as naming ceremonies, focus upon the underlying values of the culture: generosity, fortitude, and, ultimately, compassion. However, most of the male ritualists assume greater importance in these rituals, as do the males who are "pierced" in the Sun Dance. Recently, women have offered bits of skin from their arms, but this is a recent innovation.

It is also important to examine the views and attitudes of native men. Some Sioux males, for example, readily admit that they are chauvinistic and that they like this state of affairs. Others give lip service to the old traditions and the complementarity of the sexes. Some are decidedly profemale and orient their daughters toward leadership roles, both in the indigenous and the dominant societal contexts. This may account for the fact that Standing Rock reservation had two Tribal Chairwomen in the 1940s and 1950s. Only recently has there been another Chairwoman in another reservation (Lower Brule). The few Lakota males who consciously train their daughters for leadership roles are not in the ascendancy, however. This encouraging attitude was more characteristic of a previous generation. There is, nonetheless, a strong core of Lakota women who are in positions of influence, both on and off the reservations.

Why, then, do some women adhere to the ideology of male superiority as embodied in the concept of bloka? To some, it is a tradition that is needed to validate their "Indian-ness." To others, the commitment is essential inside the tribal community, while a more aggressive and assertive style is more in keeping with the interactions outside the native community. To others, the ideology emphasizes sacrifice or the more commonly-used phrase "helping my people." Whatever the perception, the process most often involves female subordination. Traditional socialization along gender lines also is an important consideration.

When one examines native ideologies, one often finds that they are built upon divinely-sanctioned controls. These native charters are often utilized to revamp symbols and maintain the status quo.

Many recent statements from Indian males almost mirror the statements of males in the Black Power movements of the 1960s. Many of the adherents of the American Indian Movement (AIM) have indicated that their goal to promote "Indian unity" is "to have a girl in every tribe." Still other males adroitly manipulate the notion of "commitment" to Indian causes to involvements that ensure the birth of children. The production of children is also seen by males and some females as a means of combatting the genocidal actions of the federal government, thus the tremendous outcry at the sterilization of American Indian women and at the difficulty of obtaining accurate information about its extent. Both native American males and females are concerned about the ethnocidal and genocidal practices that have been the lot of American Indians.

There are other areas where contemporary Indian women are pressured to conform to the native ideology. One concerns the factor of intermarriage with non-Indians. The implication of Lesbianism or frigidity is a powerful means of soliciting sexual favors from women often resorted to by Indian men. Besides decrying professional women as "Women's Libbers," many native men attempt to control female activism by indicating that "we know what she needs" (sexual encounters of a native sort, of course!). Many native women allow themselves to be manipulated in this way. Contemporary Indian sexuality has not been researched in an adequate fashion. Aspects of homosexuality — traditional patterns and also manifestations in the present day — have only begun to be examined.(11)

That pressures to conform to "tribal norms," — that is, to marry native men — are strong is noticeable in the disproportionate numbers of professional women, now divorced, who were previously married to white men. Another observation indicates that some professional native women have married native men whom they met while teaching classes in prisons. The impact of intermarriage and miscegenation is also blurred at present, but is an important consideration relating to "Indian identity."

Affirmative action also has a biological basis as far as native women are concerned. This is especially true in the academic arena where many tenure positions are occupied by individuals (males and females) who claim Indian ancestry.

Thus, it might be best to end this chapter by stressing that the ideological bases for tribal women are varied and need to be delineated. Perhaps the most common themes running through tribal histories are cultural suppression and racism. To analyze how tribal women have coped with this in association with study of the male and female ethos and world views reflective of native gender ideologies would add much to the comprehension of American Indian women of today.

NOTES

(1) John Blakeless, The Eyes of Discovery (New York: Dover Publications, 1961).

(2) See also Joseph Epes Brown, ed., The Sacred Pipe: Black Elk's Account of the Seven Rites of the Oglala Sioux (Norman: University of Oklahoma Press, 1964).

(3) Royal B. Hassrick, The Sioux, Life and Customs of a Warrior Society (Norman: University of Oklahoma Press, 1964).

(4) John Fire/Lame Deer and Richard Erdoes, Lame Deer: Seeker of Visions (New York: Simon and Schuster, Touchstone Book, 1972), pp. 253-254.

(5) Beatrice Medicine, unpublished field notes, 1979.

(6) Mary Douglas, Purity and Danger, An Analysis of Concepts of Pollution (Baltimore: Penguin Books, 1966).

(7) Ella Deloria, Speaking of Indians (New York: Friendship Press, 1945), pp. 39-40.

(8) Eleanor Leacock, "Matrifocality in a Simple Hunting Society (Montagnais-Naskapi)," Southwestern Journal of Anthropology 11 (1955): 31-47.

(9) Laila Shukry Hamamsy, "The Role of Women in a Changing Navajo Society," American Anthropologist 59 (1957): 101-111.

(10) Irene Stewart, A Voice in Her Tribe, A Navajo Woman's Own Story (Socorro, NM: Ballena Press, 1980).

(11) Beatrice Medicine, "Changing Sex Roles in an Urban Context: Native Americans," Paper presented to the Central States Anthropological Society, Milwaukee, 1979.

Figure VII. Garment Worker, Long Island City, New York. Photograph by Earl Dotter/American Labor.

6
The Scientific Mystique: Can a White Lab Coat Guarantee Purity in the Search for Knowledge about the Nature of Women? *

KAREN MESSING

In the last hundred years science has been the most important avenue for validating myths about women's nature. Cloaked in "scientific objectivity," scientists have made pronouncements about women which have largely reflected prevailing social ideas. In this chapter, Karen Messing shows in detail how social biases affect the outcome of supposedly disinterested scientific research.

In the 1950s and 1960s, Yale professor, Stanley Milgram, reported results from a series of experiments which shocked many academics.(1) In these experiments he asked his subjects to press a button which they believed delivered painful electric shocks to people, in an ostensible attempt to find out how much electricity the human body could stand. The "victims" were confederates of the experimenter and simulated increasing pain and anguish as the subjects thought they were intensifying the shocks. To Milgram's surprise, 20% of the subjects could be induced to administer "shocks" that they believed were lethal, when told by the experimenter that the study required it. And if the investigator wore a lab coat, the percentage of "killer" subjects who would do this increased to 65%. These experiments were commonly interpreted as showing that people are very obedient to authority. It is clear that they also demonstrate the tremendous respect lay people have for the authority of scientists and for scientific experiments.

Part of this scientific "mystique" comes from the image of science as the search for objective truth, a pursuit of knowledge carried out in neutral surroundings by disinterested observers. This view is based on a

*I would like to thank Lesley Lee for bringing the methodological issues in the mathematics and sex research to my attention, and Jean-Pierre Reveret and Luc Desnoyers for reading the manuscript. Funds were provided by the Institutional Research Fund of the Universite du Quebec a Montreal.

romanticism that most scientists do not actively discourage, but which has, as all of us who do science know, very little to do with reality.

In the present chapter I will show that the scientific community is in fact molded by the society of which it is a part. Scientists, and the data we produce, are not and cannot be free from the prejudices, ideologies, or interests of the larger society. This lack of objectivity is manifested in the ways scientists are selected and in the scientific results themselves. The examples I use will relate primarily to the treatment of women(2) by the scientific community, but similar mechanisms affect working-class people, Blacks, or any other group that is under-represented in the scientific establishment.

It will be useful to look at several components of the scientific process; they can be divided roughly into those relating to the scientists themselves and those pertaining to the process.

The scientist
  1. The selection of scientists
  2. Their access to facilities for scientific work.
I will show that research scientists are a highly selected group whose interests are not typical of a cross section of society. This situation has a strong influence on the scientific process.

The process

  3. The choice of research topic
  4. The wording of the hypothesis
  5. The choice of experimental subjects
  6. The choice of appropriate controls
  7. The method of observation
  8. Data analysis
  9. The interpretation of data
 10. The publication of results
 11. The popularization of results
For each of these components, I will give examples of how the ideology and background of the researcher can influence the results and how these results then become accepted scientific truth.

THE SELECTION OF THE SCIENTIST

Many articles have been written lately on the difficulties facing women who want to be scientists. These barriers have been of various kinds: exploitation of women scientists,(3) undervaluing of their contributions,(4) and exclusion of them from "old-boy" communication networks.(5)

In addition, many women are cut off at the start by the forced choice between childbearing and graduate studies.(6) It usually takes eight to nine years of post-secondary education to get a Ph.D. in the sciences. For a person to get through this, he or she must have a great deal of persistence and confidence and either a good supply of money or the time to earn it. Financial needs go up and available time, of course, goes down when childcare is involved. The demands of research can produce major conflicts for those of us with children. Chemical reactions, physical phenomena, and cell behavior do not fit neatly into an eight hour day. Therefore, the laboratory scientist must be available at all hours and often on weekends. The same is true of field work in ecology or geology, for example.

For this reason, conciliation of research schedules with childbearing and childraising is nearly impossible to do well. At 5 P.M., just as one has finally got conditions for an experiment right, it is time to pick up the children. One has the unacceptable choices of rushing off to the day-care center, thereby wasting the day's work or making the phone calls to the day-care center, arranging a sitter, changing the arrangements for supper, and staying to do the experiment and afterward facing one's own guilt and the eventual revenge of children and mate. The total exhaustion associated with this period is not conducive to creative work of any kind.(7) One of my graduate students supports her two children, aged 1 and 2, by taking part-time jobs. By the time she gets to the lab in the morning, she feels she has already put in a full work day.

The scientific community does not tolerate the temporary lowering of productivity associated with childraising, although the years of graduate studies are also those in which most people have children. The Canadian NSERC fellowships for gifted students have an absolute limit of two years in which to obtain the Master of Sciences degree. While maternity leave (unpaid) is granted, no provision is made for a slower rhythm of work once the mother returns to the laboratory or field. If she takes longer than two years for the M.Sc., she can get no Ph.D. support.

These conditions make it equally difficult for anyone to hold a part-time job, so that the student who must earn money in order to stay in school faces the same problem as someone with family responsibilities.

ACCESS TO FACILITIES FOR SCIENTIFIC WORK

Doing science requires space, equipment, and infrastructure. While some world-shaking results have been obtained using minimal facilities, most modern biological endeavors, for example, are facilitated by the latest models of spectrophotometers, computer-assisted chromatography, scintillation counters, ultracentrifuges, and so on. Plenty of these machines are found in the top rated universities, where up-and-coming scientists are hired to tenure track positions if they have been superstars in graduate school. Less successful scientists are found in underequipped universities and in less secure jobs, where even access to a laboratory may be a problem.

In the United States, female Ph.D.'s are more than four times as likely as males to be unemployed and constitute only 6.6% of tenured

Ph.D. faculty in the sciences. Most of the scientific community is now white and male.(8) This is not to say that Blacks or females necessarily would do neutral, non-sexist research, but that science is done primarily by only certain people, who seek recognition from peers who are similar to them.

THE CHOICE OF RESEARCH TOPIC

The choice of topic is influenced by several factors: the interest of the scientist, that of his or her present and future employers, and the ability to get funding for the work. Because of their sex and class, the large majority of scientists are less likely than the general population to be interested in such topics as the occupational exposures that present a risk to the nursing mother, alternate (non-hormonal) treatments for the discomforts of menopause, how a woman can give herself a safe (and, where necessary, secret) abortion, what work postures increase the likelihood of menstrual cramps, and how a low-income family can provide itself with nutritious meals. On the other hand, there is plenty of research, supported by drug companies, on drug therapy for menopausal women,(9) by government on what racial and income groups have the most abortions,(10) by employers on the relationship between women's physiological cycles and productivity,(11) and by private charity on how to prevent a rich fat-laden diet from causing heart disease.(12)

THE WORDING OF THE RESEARCH HYPOTHESIS

Articulating the hypothesis is crucial to the scientific method. Research is done in order to find an answer to a specific question, and the way the question is posed often determines the way the research will be carried out and how the eventual data will be interpreted. John Money and Anke Ehrhardt, for example, have done a good deal of research on whether prenatal hormone exposures explain sex-specific behaviors. In one study(13) they looked at children who have only one sex chromosome, an X, rather than the usual two (XX for girls, XY for boys), a condition that is called Turner's syndrome and is symbolized XO. Money and Ehrhardt hypothesized that since XO children, like normal girls, are less exposed than males to prenatal androgens (so-called male hormones) they should be "feminine," just as normal XX girls are. They defined "femininity" as not being a tomboy, preferring "girls' toys," wearing dresses rather than pants, being marriage-oriented rather than career-oriented in early adolescence, and so forth. By these criteria, their XO subjects were indeed found to be even more feminine than normal XX girls. It is unlikely that an investigator who was less accepting of present day sex role stereotypes would have shaped the hypothesis this way, since she or he would consider "femininity" an inappropriate variable on which to study individuals with Turner's syndrome, who, though they have a vulva and not a penis, in fact lack most primary and all secondary female sexual characteristics. They are further distinguished by being unusually short, and many have a webbed neck and are mentally retarded. Hence, they probably have quite different social and biological experiences than most ordinary girls. A more critical investigator might also question the criteria of "femininity" chosen by these authors.

The controversy surrounding XYY males a few years ago is a similar example of a hypothesis that was based on a socially-defined point of view, this time involving prejudice about males. Early investigators, finding a large number of men with an extra male (Y) chromosome in prisons, formulated the hypothesis that people who have an extra Y chromosome (XYY) must be "supermales," which they took to mean that these people would be especially prone to violence. They failed to consider the fact that XYY males often are unusually large, slow, and somewhat retarded. Thus, it was only after much money and time had been wasted that another hypothesis, that XYY males had the same chance as other retarded males of being in prison, was tested and confirmed.(14)

THE CHOICE OF EXPERIMENTAL SUBJECTS

The clearest example of bias in the choice of a study population is the simple and extremely common exclusion of women from studies in which one wishes to obtain information about people. In a study of occupational cancers in the lead industry, all 950 women (but not Blacks or short people) were excluded in order to keep the sample uniform.(15) In another study, as reported by Jeanne Stellman, 370,599 males were studied by the National Institutes of Health, in order to identify risk factors for heart disease.(16) Heart disease is also the leading cause of death in women, but women's risk factors were not studied. In reporting the results of such studies, authors rarely state clearly that they apply only to men.

Another way that a poor image of women (especially poor Third World women) conditions research strategies is by a callous disregard for the welfare of female subjects. For example, the birth control pill, though developed in Massachusetts, was first tested in Puerto Rico. And in 1971, long after its efficacy had been established, Dr. Joseph Goldzieher decided to test the Pill once more at his clinic. Without their knowledge, eighty of his 398 patients were given placebos (pills that looked and tasted like the Pill but were ineffective) instead of the Pill. All of the women chosen for this study had proven themselves fertile by having at least three previous children. Within a few months, ten of the women who were receiving the fake pills had become pregnant with unwanted fetuses(17)! Legal abotion was not available for these women.

THE CHOICE OF APPROPRIATE CONTROLS

The choice of controls is probably the factor that has the most influence on research results. Our research group was recently confronted with this issue when trying to determine whether rates of congenital malformations were higher than usual among the offspring of men occupationally exposed to a radioactive dust. These men lived near the factory, which discharged its untreated effluent into the air. If we used neighbors as controls, we would underestimate the effects of factory-caused exposures, since both groups would have some exposure to the dust. If we used as controls people who lived elsewhere, the measured effect might be greater, but we would be unable to identify the proportion due to specifically occupational exposures. Yet the usefulness of the results in bargaining with employers might be enhanced, because of the greater difference between the workers and the unexposed control population.

A glaring example of a poor choice of control group comes from a study of the effects of occupational exposure to radium.(18) Sharpe examined the incidence of stillbirths and miscarriages among female workers exposed to radium and compared them to pregnancy outcomes of the wives of their male coworkers, calling this "a not unreasonable control group." Not unreasonable, that is, if one forgets that males can also suffer genetic damage from radium exposure and pass it on to their children. The common idea that child bearing is an exclusively female province may account for Sharpe's forgetfulness.

Another example of the selection of a control group by sex-biased assumptions occurred at a seminar given in 1977 at the Universite du Quebec by an ethologist from the Universite de Rennes in France. The speaker described a study of the mating behavior of large mammals, in which three female goats, sheep, or cows were tethered in separate stalls and offered serially to 100 males. The subsequent pawing, sniffing, and copulatory behavior of the males was recorded. When asked why 100 males were necessary, the speaker replied that it was necessary to observe the full range of behavior. When asked why, in that case, there were only three females, he answered, "To keep the conditions standard." In studying that most bilateral of behaviors, sexual intercourse, a feminist would find it less reasonable to select females to represent "standard conditions" and males to study the "range of behavior." She would assume that results would be as skewed by the choice of a limited number of individuals of one sex as of the other.

THE METHOD OF OBSERVATION

The data an investigator collects are affected by the choice of tools (questionnaires, interview schedules, observations, biochemical tests) and the data that are considered valid and relevant. Ideology can affect all of these.

For example, in their study of the prevalence of warts among poultry slaughter-house workers, Mergler, Vezina and Beauvais(19) recorded the incidence by asking workers on a questionnaire how many warts they had. The study showed that workers who reported that they worked with saws, that their workplace was humid, and/or that their protective gloves did not fit correctly, had a significantly higher incidence of warts. During a presentation of these results at a scientific meeting, the study was criticized on the basis that the workers were incompetent to count their warts and that counting should be done by a qualified medical practitioner. This criticism ignored the fact that doctors are in general less familiar with these warts than are the affected workers, some of whom had upwards of a hundred warts on their hands.

Crucial data can also be ignored because of ideological bias. In a 1963 study of the effect of work on pregnancy outcome by the US Public Health Service, the worker's husband's occupation was recorded, but that of the pregnant worker herself was not.(20) This expensive study was thus useless for identifying working conditions that pose a risk to pregnant women and their fetuses, and the absence of such data has rendered protection very difficult.(21) Nevertheless, a recent (1980) study of the causes of premature delivery did not even include in its parameters the question of whether the mother was employed, let alone her particular occupation.(22) The bias that blinds investigators to the fact that many married women work outside the home prevents research results from helping employed women.

A methodological weakness found in many studies of sex-specific behavior is the reliance on a single observer who is aware of the hypothesis being tested, and who may therefore be biased. The Money and Ehrhardt studies(23) for example, compared girls of various hormonal statuses with respect to "femininity" on the basis of an interview with a single counselor who knew the girl's history. Another example of a single-observer study comes from sociobiology. David Barash formulated the hypothesis that male ducks rape females because the males need to ensure a maximal number of descendants to maximize their own "reproductive success." Based on this, he predicted that a female who had been raped by a strange male would be reraped as soon as possible by her usual consort (ducks live in couples). To test this complex hypothesis, Barash (alone) observed mallards for 558 hours, decided (alone) which male ducks were "husbands" and which were "strangers," and also which copulations were rape and which were mutually desired. He found, unsurprisingly, that his observations squared with his hypothesis.(24)

Even when experiments are performed under controlled laboratory conditions, observers may be biased by their political or social interests. A technical study of the chromosomes (hereditary materials) of people exposed to industrial pollutants ran into this problem. For many years, the Hooker Chemical company discharged waste products into Love Canal, New York. Residents noticed a high rate of congenital malformations and illness among their children and pets and asked the

Environmental Protection Agency to do a study. Eleven of 37 residents were found to have abnormal looking chromosomes. When the residents demanded to be evaluated, a review panel was set up to look at the chromosomes. The panel did not see the same abnormalities as the EPA.(25) Thus started a long exchange in the pages of scientific journals. Each side has its scientists, but the scientists on the two sides did not perceive the chromosomes on the microscope slides in the same way.

DATA ANALYSIS

There is a large literature on "demand characteristics" of experimental situations; that is, the tendency of experimenters, their subjects, and their research assistants to produce by unconscious manipulations the data desired by the investigator.(26) Steven Gould has illustrated this point in his reanalysis of data on cranial capacity of different races, showing how a distinguished nineteenth century investigator manipulated his data to prove (incorrectly) that Blacks had smaller brains than whites.(27) Another study of experimenter bias showed that research assistants made three times as many errors in arithmetic that favored the chief's hypothesis as errors that went against it.(28)

Few nonscientists are aware of how many simple errors can be found in the scientific literature and in well-known, respected journals. For instance, the previously cited Money and Ehrhardt article used a statistical (chi-square) test under conditions where the use of this test is forbidden by elementary statistics texts (too many expected values were less than five). The Barash study contained an arithmetic error that rendered results statistically significant, in that the probability of the situation occurring by chance is given as less than .001, when the data in fact yield a probability of its occurring through chance alone as greater than .05.

There are also instances of intentional misanalyses of data. A case that has recently come to light is that of Sir Cyril Burt, a prominent British psychologist and educational planner, who is now known to have manipulated data supposedly collected from twins reared apart so as to demonstrate a strong genetic component in IQ.(29) The fact that it took nearly 50 years for Burt's deceptions to be revealed is perhaps evidence that his conclusions, used for many years to argue for racial and class differences in intelligence, agreed so closely with widely held prejudices, that a critical eye was never cast on the data.

THE INTERPRETATION OF DATA

One of the major questions in the occupational health and safety field, as well as in the anti-nuclear movement, is the degree of genetic damage induced by low levels of ionizing radiation. In Quebec, a case is under arbitration in which a radiodiagnostic technician applied for leave with pay during her pregnancy in accordance with a contract clause that provides for such leave if working conditions endanger a fetus. The employer argued that radiation below a certain threshold level poses no problem for the fetus; the union argued that there is no threshold, and that any exposure is associated with some probability of damage.(30) Scientists were found to testify on both sides, since the argument turns on the extrapolation of a particular dose-responsive curve, for which it is prohibitively time consuming and expensive to obtain complete data to the lowest possible doses.(31, 32) Scientists testifying on behalf of the union or the employer interpreted the same data in opposite ways; each found that the data supported the contention of her or his side.

There are many such cases where interpretation of data depends on one's point of view; the controversies about race and IQ,(33) about male "genes" for mathematical ability,(34) and about the effectiveness of chemical spraying in insect control(35) are examples of areas where an intensive research effort has not succeeded in settling a scientific question, due to the involvement of opposing groups with a vested economic or social interest in opposite conclusions.

THE PUBLICATION OF RESULTS

After writing up the research results, the scientist submits a paper to a journal, which sends it to a few people working in the same field for review. This process is meant to guarantee that no slipshod work is published, that errors will be corrected, and that worthy articles find an audience. In practice the system is far from ideal. Once a scientist has made a name, he or she (though, of course, usually he) can often get an article published quickly after only perfunctory review. Less well-known scientists can have considerably more difficulty, especially if their results depart from accepted dogma.

Results that reinforce prevalent biases are often accepted without question. For example, last year, the anthropologist C. O. Lovejoy published an article in Science with the ambitious title, "The Origin of Man."(36) Some weeks later, he informed journalists that he had played a little joke. He had stated in his discussion that "the human female is continually sexually receptive." As authority for this statement he cited not research results, but "D. C. Johannsen, personal communication." This is the learned equivalent of saying, "My buddy told me in the locker room." Presumably because the original statement did not seem unreasonable to the reviewers, none of them picked up the faulty citation. A feminist reviewer might have, of course.

THE POPULARIZATION OF RESULTS

Many research papers have been published on the cause of superior male performance on mathematics tests in high school.(37) Some papers support the hypothesis that males have superior genes, others that they have an environmentally conferred advantage. Therefore, it is hard to find a scientific basis for the fuss and furor which followed the publication of a recent study by Benbow and Stanley showing that one proposed environmental determinant – number of mathematics courses taken – could be eliminated from consideration.(38) There was no attempt by the authors to eliminate all environmental influences, and no evidence for genetic determination was offered. Yet the paper elicited editorial comment in the issue of Science magazine in which it appeared, and within a few weeks of publication Time, Newsweek, and local newspapers were publishing articles with titles like "Sex differences in achievement in and attitudes toward mathematics result from superior mathematical ability."(39) No similar publicity had accompanied Elizabeth Fennema's article of a few years earlier,(40) in which, based on the same data, she had argued for an environmental determination. The ideology of the media greatly influences which scientific results enter into the popular culture.

Some results lend themselves to use in political and social battles. Money and Ehrhardt's research on hormonal determination of sex-typical behavior has slipped into the givens of popular science. They are quoted extensively in the sexology courses at the Universite du Quebec and in popular magazine articles.(41)

And David Barash, after studying rape in birds, wrote a widely read Psychology Today article in which he suggested that the double standard of sexual behavior among humans follows the bird pattern, due to men's biologically-based need to inject their sperm into as many women as possible.(42) This view was also quickly picked up and published by Playboy, under the title, "Do Men Need to Cheat on Their Women? A New Science Says Yes."(43)

On the other hand, ideology and special interests may prevent some research results from becoming publicized. In 1979, Dr. David Horrobin was fired from the Clinical Research Institute of Montreal for having "prematurely" publicized research results suggesting that the tranquilizer valium may promote cancer of the breast in women. These results, subsequently confirmed by other investigators, were certainly of immediate practical value for women, since one woman in eleven gets breast cancer and valium is the most commonly used prescription drug on the market.(44) No such censorship has been practiced on Benbow's and Stanley's results or interpretations, which are prejudicial to women's education, on those of Barash, which justify rape, or on those of Burt, which support racism, although Horrobin's studies were based on much more data than any of these.

In fact, as we have seen in the preceding examples, scientists, protected by their image as zealous seekers after truth, have been allowed to say the most outrageous things about women with impunity. Such statements have been used to limit women's access to educational and occupational opportunities and have damaged our health. And, of course, scientists have also done damage to minority and working class men. The problem of scientific objectivity is therefore not simply an academic one.

It is about time that scientists be regarded with the same skepticism as other members of the establishment. If and when we achieve an egalitarian society, we may hope for a science more in touch with people's needs. Industrial hygienists will listen to workers when they look for risks associated with working conditions. Biologists will consult with, rather than experiment on, women who want contraceptive devices, and psychologists will search for the basis of cooperative rather than aggressive behavior. Until that time, since we still have a long struggle ahead of us, we would be wise to examine closely, even belligerently, what scientists have to say about the nature of women.

NOTES

(1) Stanley Milgram, Obedience to Authority (New York: Harper & Row, 1973).

(2) The treatment of women is more specifically covered in Ruth Hubbard, Mary Sue Henifin and Barbara Fried, eds., Biological Woman – The Convenient Myth (Cambridge, Mass.: Schenkman Publishing Co., 1982). This book contains an extensive bibliography.

(3) Naomi Weisstein, "Adventures of a Woman in Science," Fed. Proc. 35 (1976): 2226-2231.

(4) Anne Sayre, Rosalind Franklin and DNA: A Vivid View of What It Is Like to be a Gifted Woman in an Especially Male Profession (New York: W. W. Norton and Co., 1975).

(5) Nancy Hopkins, "The High Price of Success in Science," Radcliffe Quarterly 62 (June 1976): 16-18.

(6) Liliane Stehelin, "Science, Women and Ideology," in Ideology of/in the Natural Sciences, H. Rose and S. Rose, eds. (Cambridge, Mass.: Schenkman Publishing Co., 1979).

(7) I speak from my own experience and that of my graduate students.

(8) Betty Vetter, "Degree Completion by Women and Minorities in Science Increases," Science 214 (1982): 1313-1321; Betty M. Vetter and Elinor L. Babco, "New Data Show Slow Changes in Science Labor Force," Science 216 (1982): 1094-1095.

(9) M. Whitehead et al., "Systemic Absorption from Premarin Vaginal Cream," in I. D. Cooke, ed., The Role of Estrogen/Progesterone in the Management of the Menopause (Baltimore, Md.: University Park Press, 1978).

(10) Center for Disease Control, Abortion Surveillance, 1978. (Issued November 1980. U. S. Department of Health and Human Services.)

(11) F.S. Preston et al., "Effects of Flying and of Time Changes on Menstrual Cycle Length and on Performance in Airline Stewardesses," Aerospace Medicine 44 (1973): 438-443.

(12) A. Kurkis et al., "Effect of Saturated and Unsaturated Fat Diets on Lipid Profiles of Plasma Lipoproteins," Atherosclerosis 41 (1982): 221-241.

(13) Anke Ehrhardt, Nancy Greenberg, and John Money, "Female Gender Identity and Absence of Fetal Gonadal Hormones: Turner's Syndrome," Johns Hopkins Medical Journal 126 (1970): 237-248.

(14) Herman A. Witkin et al., "Criminality in XYY and XXY Men," Science 193 (1976): 547-555.

(15) W. Clarke Cooper, "Cancer Mortality Patterns in the Lead Industry," Annals N.Y. Acad. Sci. 271 (1976): 2250-259.

(16) Jeanne M. Stellman, Women's Work, Women's Health: Myths and Realities (New York: Pantheon Books, 1977), pp. 32-33.

(17) Gena Corea, The Hidden Malpractice (New York: HBJ Books, 1977), p. 16.

(18) William D. Sharpe, "Chronic Radium Intoxication: Clinical and Autopsy Findings in Long-term New Jersey Survivors," Environmental Research 8 (1974): 243-383, 310.

(19) Donna Mergler, Nicole Vezina, and Annette Beauvais, "Warts Amongst Workers in Poultry Slaughter-houses," Scand. J. of Work, Envi. and Health 8, suppl. 1 (1982): 180-184.

(20) U.S. Department of Health, Education and Welfare, Employment During Pregnancy: Legitimate Live Births 1963 (Washington, D.C.: U.S. Government Printing Office, 1963).

(21) Karen Messing, "Est-ce que la travailleuse enceinte est protegee au Quebec?" Union Medicale (February, 1982).

(22) Gertrud S. Berkowitz, "An Epidemiologic Study of Preterm Delivery," Am. J. Epidemiol. 113 (1981): 81-92.

(23) Anke A. Ehrhardt, Ralph Epstein, and John Money, "Fetal Androgens and Female Gender Identity in the Early-treated Androgenital Syndrome," Johns Hopkins Med. Journal 122 (1968): 160-168; see also study in note 13.

(24) David Barash, "Sociobiology of Rape in Mallards (Anas platyrynchos): Responses of the Mated Male," Science 197 (1977): 788-789.

(25) Gina B. Kolata, "Love Canal: False Alarm Caused by Botched Study," Science 208 (1980): 1239-1240.

(26) Robert Rosenthal, Experimenter Effects in Behavioral Research (New York: Appleton-Century-Crofts, 1966).

(27) Steven J. Gould, "Morton's Ranking of Races by Cranial Capacity," Science 200 (1978): 503-509.

(28) J.L. Kennedy and H. P. Uhoff, "Experiments on the Nature of Extrasensory Perception, III. Recording Error Criticizer of Extra-chance Scores," J. Parapsychol. 3 (1939): 226-245.

(29) D.D. Dorfman, "The Cyril Burt Question: New Findings," Science 201 (1978): 1177-1180.

(30) Arbitration hearing on the case of Mme. Adrienne Robichaud, before Judge Jean-Jacques Turcotte, Quebec, 1980-82.

(31) Charles E. Land, "Estimating Cancer Risks from Low Doses of Ionizing Radiation," Science 209 (1980): 1197-1203.

(32) John W. Gofman, Radiation and Human Health (San Francisco: Sierra Club Books, 1981).

(33) Joanna J. Ryan, "I.Q. – The Illusion of Objectivity," in Ken Richardson and David Spears, eds., Race and Intelligence (Baltimore, MD: Penguin Books, 1972): 36-55.

(34) Jon Beckwith and John Durkin, "Girls, Boys and Math," Science for the People 13, No. 5 (Sept./Oct. 1981): 6-9; 32-35.

(35) Robert Van den Bosch, The Pesticide Conspiracy (New York: Doubleday, 1978).

(36) C. Owen Lovejoy, "The Origin of Man," Science 211 (1981): 341-350.

(37) Lynn H. Fox et al., eds., Women and the Mathematical Mystique (Baltimore, MD: Johns Hopkins University Press, 1980).

(38) Camilla P. Benbow and Julian C. Stanley, "Sex Differences in Math Ability: Fact or Artifact," Science 210 (1980): 1262-1264.

(39) D.A. Williams and P. King, "Sex Differences in Achievement in and Attitudes toward Mathematics Result from Superior Mathematical Ability," Newsweek (December 15, 1980): 73.

(40) Elizabeth Fennema, "Sex-related Differences in Mathematical Achievement: Where and Why?" in L. H. Fox et al., eds., Women and

the Mathematical Mystique (Baltimore, MD: Johns Hopkins University Press, 1980).

(41) For example, Pierre Sormany, "Le Cerveau a-t-il un sexe?" L'Actualite (November 1980): 35 ff.

(42) David Barash, "Sexual Selection in Birdland," Psychology Today (March 1978): 81-86.

(43) Scot Morris, "Do Men Need to Cheat on Their Women? A New Science Say YES: Darwin and the Double Standard," Playboy (May 1978): 109 ff.

(44) Francine F. Pelletier, "La belle au bois dormant se meurt: le valium et le cancer du sein," La Vie en Rose (Juin, Juillet, Aout 1981): 33-37.

7
Feminist Analysis of Gender: A Mystique*

JOAN SMITH

Joan Smith points out some of the dangers of neglecting the differences in women's lives and concentrating only on similarities. She shows how feminists come dangerously close to the position of biological determinists. By abstracting similar behaviors from their social context in a way that leads to the appearance of a universal patriarchy, it becomes difficult to avoid a concept of "woman's nature" paralleling that created by sociobiologists and others. She shows that this view of woman's nature is not supported by the historical evidence.

During the last two decades feminist theory has attempted to account for sexual inequality while avoiding the twin hazards of biological determinism and economic reductionism. In doing so, it has increasingly called attention to the role of unwaged labor performed in the home almost exclusively by women. An area of inquiry in its own right — though one long neglected by more conventional social science — women's domestic roles drew the attention of feminist scholars because of the part these roles played in both biologism and economism.

Biological determinism, very broadly speaking, argues that women's reproductive functions are governed by biological constraints, which in turn shape their social lives. Economism, on the other hand, argues that women's subordination is the effect of the operations of the productive system and will be automatically eradicated once women play a parity role in a labor force that has succeeded in wresting away from owners the means of production.

Recent feminist scholars have argued that women's subordination, while not biological in origin, should be located in a hierarchical division of labor that was anchored in the organization of housework and childbearing and rearing. These activities are socially organized and

---

*This is a much revised version of a paper that appeared earlier under the title of "Sociobiology and Feminism: The Very Strange Courtship of Competing Paradigms," Philosophical Forum, XIII (Spring, 1982).

Figure VIII. Maids, Black River Falls, Wisconsin, c. 1905. Photograph by
Charles J. van Schaick. State Historical Society of Wisconsin.

defined, though in patterns that predate the contemporary mode of production and comprise a relatively autonomous system of social relations. This system, usually termed patriarchal, is to be distinguished from other systems of domination, principally capitalism.

The domination of women by men to the advantage of men, it is argued, exists apart from any particular economic system but always acts in concert with whatever system accompanies it. Evidence for the accuracy of this formulation was generally drawn from the experience of socialist states. If sexual inequality was ultimately tied to a capitalist mode of production, one would expect that under certain new modes of production, socialism for one, it would disappear. Yet examinations of socialist states proved this to be a vain hope.(1) Women were still charged with reproductive and domestic activities, and these in turn solidified the second class status of both the activities and the women who performed them. Men were still accorded public roles that brought them material as well as psychic success, while women – though now waged workers – continued to be relegated to the separate and unequal sphere of domesticity.

Obviously the empirical "evidence" of the failure of socialism in producing women's liberation raised once more the spectre of the theoretical viability of biological determinism. If the relations between men and women were not subject to the revolutionary changes that accompanied the transition to socialism, it could be argued that indeed there might be a strong case for biology as an explanation for the apparent permanency of unequal and hierarchical sexual relations.

This dilemma – the Scylla of economism or the Charybdis of biologism – has established the task of the more influential feminists writing today as well as of women engaged in direct political action. The task was to find out why sex role systems seemed to be conceptually and empirically independent of economic ones, while simultaneously avoiding the pitfalls of biological determinism.

In my view, such a project has been at best only minimally successful. More crucially, whatever success has been achieved in creating a theoretical distinction between gender systems and modes of production has been purchased at the price of adopting descriptive strategies that lend themselves to biological explanations. Moreover, I will argue, by adopting these strategies, feminist theorists leave intact the most objectionable aspects of economism.

Before turning to the specifics, I must make one point about scientific explanation – not just another arcane academic point, but one central to constructing explanations for women's exploitation and thus for guiding the kind of political work necessary for its eradication.

The world of theory is governed by sets of principles upon which explanations must be based. Part of those principles involves the relationship between explanation and description. How a phenomenon is described has enormous consequences for the kind of explanation that is developed about it.(2) Let me offer just one simple example. If holding a job is defined as principally a characteristic of the individual, the issue of joblessness is entirely different than if having a job is described as principally a characteristic of the political economy. The kinds of explanations offered will vary widely. Just as importantly, so will the political solutions sought for unemployment. In short, when I go about explaining something, whether the nature of unemployment or of women's subordinate roles, I have started off with a description that sets limits on the kind of explanation I will formulate. That description is fateful in the judgments I make about how the phenomenon in question will behave — what pressures I see it responding to, what accounts for its existence, and what would effectively bring about its demise.

I will argue here that a good deal of the recent feminist scholarship that has attempted to disprove biological explanations for women's subordination, while at the same time attempting to avoid what was perceived as economism, has in fact come close to achieving the opposite result. By dislodging women's roles from their specific historical relationship to the mode of production, a number of feminist authors have reverted to descriptive tactics that parallel those found in biological explanations for women's subordination. In spite of the fact that these theorists are anything but biological determinists, paradoxically they describe women's subordination in a way that makes that subordination compatible with biologism.

In what follows I will briefly sketch how sexual hierarchies are described by the most recent of biological determinists: the socio-biologists. I will not present a systematic criticism of sociobiology; this has been done very well elsewhere.(3) Rather, my purpose is simply to sketch sociobiology's conceptual tools in order to demonstrate the parallels to be found in a particular body of feminist thought. Then I will investigate the results of using these conceptual tools in feminist theory. Last, I will try to decipher why these authors have had to employ such tools and how they could be adequately replaced.

THINKING LIKE A SOCIOBIOLOGIST

As their critics have repeatedly noted, socibiologists in accounting for social behavior attempt to abstract so-called "traits" from the multiplicity of behaviors in which they are supposedly merely expressed. To a sociobiologist, the vast differences, for example, between entering the coliseum expressly to emerge as the victor over a dead opponent and trying to ski across a snow field faster than an opponent are irrelevant. Both are instances of the same thing, in this case, aggression. In short, widely diverse social behaviors are lumped together under the "traits" they are said to manifest. This aggregation is accomplished by disregarding the specific forms in which the traits are said to be encased. Thus, aggressiveness can be anything from ski racing to killing Christians: the "trait" includes everything from fighting to the death to trading on the New York Stock Exchange. The sociobiologist tries to dissociate content from specific form so as to provide a basis for a biological account of human behavior. (I might note that the kinds of metaphors sociobiologists invoke to suggest that animal behavior parallels human activities – and for which they have been seriously criticized – depend upon this descriptive tactic.)(4) It is not the metaphor, however, that is at the heart of sociobiological descriptive machinery, but rather the mistaken dissociation of "essence" from "appearance," which allows sociobiologists to lump diverse animal behaviors under common anthropomorphic descriptions.

Besides dissociating the form of a behavior from what is defined as its essence, the sociobiologist also dissociates the so-called traits from the complex set of relationships that create sets of behaviors, govern their existence, and define their meaning to social participants.

In order to see how this descriptive strategy works, we can turn to a well-known position of sociobiologist Edward O. Wilson:

> In hunter-gatherer societies, men hunt and women stay at home. This strong bias persists in most agricultural and industrial societies, and, on that ground alone, appears to have a genetic origin. . . . My own guess is that the genetic bias is intense enough to cause a substantial division of labor even in the most free and most egalitarian of future societies.(5)

For this statement to make any explanatory sense and not be a tautology, Wilson must assert that "being at home" over the course of many thousands of centuries has some common feature other than simply that this is where women are to be found. He must argue, in short, that the highly complex and infinitely variable relationships that comprise societies and distinguish one from another are extrinsic to the act of being at home. This is accomplished in the sociobiological conceptual apparatus by defining societies as no more than the sum of their parts and implying that each part can be extracted from the totality without doing substantial damage to its nature.

Since sociobiology seeks to understand the foundations of human behavior independent of the social context within which a behavior is converted into distinctive social activity, it similarly must locate the principle of historical change, not in the relationships among parts of a social totality, but in terms of the adaptive capacities of populations. That is, sociobiologists explain the existence of a social behavior in terms of the way it functions for the reproductive success of its carrier. When it ceases to be adaptive, the carriers presumably will be replaced by populations with more adaptive genetic programming. History, then, is the account of populations that emerge at given times because they carry a genetic program more efficient at producing offspring than potentially competing populations.(6) From this formulation, it should come as no surprise that for sociobiologists, history hardly exists at all. Here is what Tiger and Fox say about the matter:

> Nothing worth noting has happened in our evolutionary history since we left off hunting and took to the fields and the towns – nothing except perhaps a little selection for immunity to

epidemics, and probably not even that. "Man the hunter" is not an episode in our distant past: we are still man the hunter, incarcerated, domesticated, polluted, crowded and bemused.(7)

Of course this view of history is a direct corollary of the earlier descriptive strategies I have described. When the form in which a "trait" is carried is unimportant relative to the "trait" itself (when it doesn't matter whether one is talking about trading in stocks or killing strangers), and when the specifics of the set of relationships that give meaning to the behavior are relegated to the status of epiphenomena, then behaviors that are widely divergent across time and societies can be lumped together and defined as examples of the same thing. Sociobiologists develop their theory of history from this vantage point. For them, history is something that occurred in some distant past. History exists in the biological origins of one genotype or another.

REDUCTIONISM AND FEMINIST THOUGHT

In what I have said about the descriptive tactics invoked by socio-biologists, we can locate three major standards for describing things. First, a behavior or trait is only explicable when it is stripped of its immediate appearance, and when that appearance is not in any systematic way linked to the basic object of inquiry. Second, the residues of this stripping process – in the case of sociobiology, the "traits" – are described in such a fashion that they are independent of the social totality in which they are found, as though they had an autonomous existence. Third, the history of these stripped-down phenomena is identified with their genesis at some point in time rather than with qualitative change in the conditions to which they are subject for their existence, reproduction, and perhaps eventual demise.

The materials the sociobiologists deal with are so widely different from those of the feminist authors I will be referring to that it takes an initial leap of the imagination to see the parallels I want to emphasize. Feminist social theory has been significantly shaped by what has come to be called socialist-feminist politics. The agreed-upon agenda for the socialist-feminists (among whom I certainly count myself) was to integrate questions of sex, race, and class and, as Ros Petchesky pointed out, "for building the bridges which we see as critical between the feminist movement and Third World, anti-imperialist, and socialist revolutionary movements."(8) The reason for the hyphen, Petchesky explained, was the inability of socialist feminists to locate women "solidly and respectably in the volumes of Capital." The purpose of the dual term "Marxist-feminist" was to note that:

> production and reproduction, work and the family far from being separate territories like the moon and the sun or the kitchen and the shop, are really intimately related modes that reverberate upon one another and frequently occur in the same social, physical, and even psychic spaces.(9)

Yet the hyphen also indicates that reproduction and kinship as well as the family have, in Petchesky's words, "their own, historically determined products, material techniques, modes of organization and power relationships."(10) Further, the male dominance that characterizes this system has significant consequences for the state. Women's subordination is determined both by the mode of production and by patriarchical structures that exercise their own control on the political economy.(11)

The hyphenated character of feminist political allegiances is reflected in what Iris Young calls dual systems theory. According to this body of feminist scholarship,

> women's oppression arises from two distinct and relatively autonomous systems. The system of male domination, most often "patriarchy," produces the specific gender oppression of women.(12)

According to those feminists who subscribe to a dual systems approach to women's roles, male domination and its concomitant female subordination is a relatively autonomous system of domination — autonomous, that is, with respect to any particular social form it occurs in. The claim is that women's subordination must itself be explained in the context of particular historical structures but, as well, in its own right, without reference to these structures.

In order for this thesis of autonomy to be coherent, it must also argue that the domination of women by men across different modes of production, while varying enormously, obviously has some core aspects in common that are more important than what distinguishes sexual hierarchies in each society they are found in. Most feminists writing in this vein locate that similarity in systems of sexual and biological reproduction. One of the most influential of such accounts and certainly the most original is Gayle Rubin's.(13)

Rubin calls the universal of sexual and reproductive relations a sex-gender system. All societies, she claims, organize the biological differences between men and women into specific social arrangements. This common sex-gender system is characterized by asymmetrical exchange in which men always exchange women and not ever the other way around. Further, this sexual division of labor absolutely ensures that the interests of men, not those of women, are met in the act of exchange. According to Rubin, the particular mode of production fills in the details of the exchange, but the sex-gender system can be both conceptually and at particular historical moments empirically isolated from the mode of production.(14)

A similar conclusion is reached by Nancy Chodorow in her analysis of the subordination of women.(15) The source of male domination is not in the particulars of the society it is found in, but in the universal fact that women, rather than men, mother. This fact has profound consequences "for family structure, for relations between the sexes, for ideology about women, and for the sexual division of labor and sexual inequality both inside the family and in the nonfamilial world."(16)

For Chodorow, sex-gender systems are on the same level of abstraction as modes of production. Every society has a sex-gender system; yet in every society the sex-gender system and the mode of production compose two distinct systems, though they are "linked (and almost inextricably intertwined) in numerous ways." In our own society, the two appear to be distinct and independent of each other because, according to Chodorow,

> material production has progressively left the home, the family has been eliminated as a productive economic unit and women and men have in some sense divided the public and domestic spheres between them.(17)

Yet for all the differences between various kinds of sex-gender systems, says Chodorow, there is a multitude of similarities from which we gain useful knowledge about the subordination of women. These similarities are linked to mothering — the exclusive province of women in all known societies:

> Women's mothering is a central and defining structural feature of our society's organization of gender, and one that it has in common with all other societies . . . features of our own sexual division of labor and kinship system remain which we can tentatively characterize as universal. . . . These include women's involvement in routine daily cooking for their immediate families . . . and heterosexuality as a sexual norm and organizational principle of family organization and the structure of marriage . . . men with full adult status do not routinely care for small children.(18)

While Chodorow notes that there are substantial variations in family and kinship patterns between societies, in the long run they are "variations within a sexual and familial division of labor in which women mother."

In a much different mode, Zillah Eisenstein recognizes a system of sexual domination existing independently of the society's economy and exhibiting identical characteristics that join it with systems of male domination found in antiquity:

> There is a continuity to patriarchal history that has not existed in economic history . . . [Patriarchy] changes historically, but universal qualities of it are maintained even if they are specifically redefined.(19)

After a remarkable and truly original review of the literature on historical periods commencing in Attic Greece and continuing through feudalism to contemporary capitalism, Eisenstein concludes:

The universality of patriarchy in Western society is expressed in the sexual assignment of private and public life. Although the meaning of "public and private" changes in concrete ways, the assignment of public space to men and private space to women is continuous in Western history.(20)

Sexual hierarchies, whether in ancient Greece or midtown Manhattan, have for Eisenstein enough in common (although they admittedly differ along several dimensions) that both can be considered the same system: patriarchy. (She has no particular commitment to the term patriarchy but only to the issue it denotes, which is that within all political history, no matter how diverse, sexual hierarchy is structurally present as a relatively autonomous system.)(21)

For Eisenstein, the root of that pan-historical commonality is to be found not in biology but in the fact that "men have chosen to interpret and politically use the fact that women are the reproducers of humanity."(22) Relations of reproduction are arranged hierarchically for all of Western history, Eisenstein argues, and thus present a unified system which interacts – sometimes in a complementary fashion and sometimes in contradiction – with particular modes of production.

Heidi Hartmann's analysis of sexual hierarchies shifts the focus away from reproduction specifically to the more general hierarchical sexual division of labor. For Hartmann, like Rubin, Chodorow, and Eisenstein, sexual hierarchies where men are dominant can be located in a variety of societies:

In this perspective capitalism is a relative late comer, whereas patriarchy, the hierarchical relation between men and women in which men are dominant and women are subordinate, was an early arrival.(23)

What joins together the variety of forms in which this domination emerges is the fact that men control women's labor and because they have this control, occupy different places in kin structures than do women. This difference in kinship place is the common element running through all of postprimitive history and, according to Hartmann, it gets utilized in the organization of contemporary wage labor.

Thus, for each of the theorists I have been discussing (and they represent some of the most serious and interesting of recent feminist scholarship) female subordination cannot be reduced to or explained by the mode of production because it shares common and central features with female subordination as found in a variety of productive systems. Men in all societies have control over the exchange of women (Rubin); women do the mothering, which sets up asymmetrical and exploitative relationships between men and women (Chodorow); no political revolution has yet addressed itself to patriarchal relations, so men dominate women in whatever social formation emerges by continually relegating them to private spheres (Eisenstein); and male control over female labor can be put to any number of uses in a variety of social contexts

(Hartmann). The analysis of male domination and female subordination rests on the author's assigning near universality to one or another social arrangement. The semblance of universality of male dominance arises from the strategy of divesting its core features of the vast panoply of social arrangements that give it its actual, temporal forms. Once these arrangements are peeled away, the dazzling variety of relationships subsumed under the term "male domination" become examples of essentially the same thing. The bride price in an ancient African tribe and the twentieth century marriage contract that stipulates mutual obligations should the relationship dissolve are treated merely as different examples of the same core social relationship of domination.

The attempt to elucidate a central core or essence of male domination is part of the more general effort to explain what is seen as its regularity. This attempt rests on a commonly held assumption concerning the nature of human social relationships and the sort of descriptive tactics that must be employed to grasp and explain them adequately. Specifically, from the point of view of the feminist accounts I have described here, it is assumed that any relationship must be described in such a manner as to get beyond its immediate features and reach its essence. Though always shrouded in the particularities of the moment, it is as though this essence, rather than the contemporary setting it is found in, determines the way male domination makes its appearance on the historical stage.

Because a principal feature of male supremacy, as it is described in much of contemporary feminist theory, is its putative autonomy from any particular known historical period, it exists in a semi-isolation chamber. Its connection to any other feature of social life is not an essential dimension of its nature. It is this aspect of the conceptual apparatus employed by many feminist theorists that allows them to suggest that partiarchy is at once a precondition for the modern period and something that could outlive it.

Here, for example, is how Hartmann describes this feature of patriarchy:

> A schematic view of the development of capitalism in Western societies suggests that capitalism generally took root in societies where production and redistribution had taken place largely in households and villages. . . . The decentralized home system, which I see as a fundamental result of patriarchy, also meets crucial requirements for the reproduction of the capitalist system.(24)

I have no quarrel with Hartmann's important observation that the development of the decentralized home as the locus of production, distribution, and exchange was an important ingredient in the early accumulation necessary for the formation of capital.(25) I also have no problem with the observation that a decentralized home meets the requirements for reproducing the capitalist wage relationship. But Hartmann is saying more than just that, and this is what I wish to direct the reader's attention to.

In Hartmann's formulation quoted above, the home she refers to is the key site of the hierarchical nature of the relationship between men and women. With respect to key aspects of male domination, such as control over production and reproduction, that "home" is no different under advanced capitalism than under the stage of primitive accumulation. Indeed, she argues elsewhere, the continuation of this domestic hierarchical relationship between men and women was won by working class men in the face of what would have otherwise been different tendencies of capital in "its pure form."(26)

But to identify precapitalist households with contemporary ones is in my view to obscure precisely what we need to know about female subordination.

The period of capitalist primitive accumulation to which Hartmann refers was that period in which accumulation of capital took place on the basis of relationships of production that were precapitalist. In that sense, the disaggregated and independent households to which Hartmann properly draws our attention were a precondition for the development of full capitalist production, but they were not yet capitalist themselves. The outcome of that primitive accumulation is part of a world-wide historical process that eventually led to the dominance of the capital wage relation as the guiding principle in the entire world economy. That wage relationship exercises its influence over all relations, even though they may concretely fall outside of the wage. Once that occurred and nonhousehold labor became preeminent, activities within the household became ordered by a set of relationships totally different from and in opposition to those that had been at work in the earlier period. That is, household labor and the set of relationships to which it is subject became an <u>outcome</u> of the capitalist wage relationship and no longer its presupposition.(27)

Depending on historical circumstances, household labor, along with the set of household relationships that guaranteed it and gave it form, have had entirely different kinds of determinants and articulations with the rest of the social world through the ages. No matter how similar they may look on the surface, the relationships between men and women now and six centuries ago are not only different, they are antithetical. It was precisely the overthrow of family-located obligations and responsibilities for production and the rise of individualism that were the preconditions for the full development of the capitalist wage relationship. If we fail to grasp this fact, and instead lump all relationships between men and women over the centuries into the catch-all category of patriarchy, we ensure that we will totally misunderstand the most crucial aspect of women's history. We will, in fact, render women's history nonexistent. <u>The determinants that were responsible for the existence of household labor and the existence of the set of social relationships it expresses during the stage of primitive accumulation were undermined at every step precisely by the role those relationships played in the development of capitalist production.</u> They were replaced by a set of determinants that were the antithesis of earlier ones. By suggesting that capital "borrowed" patriarchical relationships located in and expressed by the organization of families and households, Hartmann dismisses this central historical process as largely irrelevant to the hierarchical relationships between men and women.

A similar analytical stance is adopted by Eisenstein in her analysis of what she calls "capitalist patriarchy":

> patriarchy precedes capitalism through the existence of the sexual ordering of society which derives from ideological and political interpretations of biological differences . . . a patriarchical culture is carried over from one historical period to another to protect the sexual hierarchy of society. . . . A sexual division of labor and society that defines people's activities, purposes, goals, desires, and dreams according to their biological sex, is at the base of patriarchy and capitalism. It divides men and women into their respective hierarchical sex roles and structures their related duties in the family domain and within the economy.(28)

If patriarchy in Eisenstein's formulation is to mean anything more than an abstract concept that captures the infinite variety of arrangements assumed by the biological raw material of sex, she must mean that some specific set of conditions for the domination of women by men is imported from one mode of production to another. Yet Eisenstein fails to specify what material conditions give life to the ideas and beliefs that make men "choose" to dominate women. Such specification is essential in order to validate real and objective sexual oppression. We can choose to do almost anything, but unless we have access to the socially organized conditions necessary to be effective, our "choices" will hardly meet with success. I could choose to dominate my dean, for example, but the effort would probably result in something other than what I had intended.

Old ideas of domination and beliefs of women's sexual inferiority can persist only if there are real material conditions that place men and women in unequal and hierarchical relationships to each other.(29) These relationships can remain both unequal and hierarchical and still be fundamentally altered by virtue of changes in the conditions that guarantee their continued existence as well as in the specific set of constraints and contradictions to which they are subject. If Eisenstein is to be accurate in her assessment that patriarchy is a system distinct from the mode of production, both the conditions of its reproduction and its contradictions must in all relevant respects be identical across different economic systems. Nevertheless, since she insists that patriarchy can be considered apart from any specific organization of material life, these material relationships are never delineated.(30)

Social relationships – the backbone of our ideas and actions – are fundamentally defined and ordered by the set of processes responsible for their origination, reproduction, and possible demise. As capitalist social relations took hold throughout the world, relationships emerged between men and women that were increasingly and integrally linked with capitalist-dominated production and the distribution and consumption of capitalist commodities. These relationships were subject to entirely new constraints and contradictions. Ideas that predated capitalism persisted not because the grounds of the earlier relationships between men and women persisted, but because these ideas served to shore up new relationships and protect them from new constraints.

Feminists must address themselves to historical processes, not only in constructing adequate theories of female subordination, but perhaps more importantly in political struggles. Yet it is precisely these processes that are obscured in feminist accounts of male domination when theorists abstract domination from the distinct set of relations that are responsible for reproducing it and treat it as separate from the set of socially structured and historically specific constraints and contradictions to which contemporary male domination is liable.

By assuming that the infinite variety of activities women were assigned over the past amounted to essentially the same experience, and by further assuming that the wide variety of relationships with which male-domination and female-subordination were articulated over many centuries are unrelated to the core fact of women's less-than-equal status, many feminists have increasingly treated sexual hierarchies as though their historical breadth were far wider than that of any specific mode of production. Indeed, for some feminist writers, these relationships have amounted to a universal fact of human experience.(31) It is this putative supra-historical quality that demands explanation for a good many feminists writing today and has set up what Rosaldo recently criticized as a search for origins.(32) Yet in my view this near universality, rather than being a historical fact that needs to be accounted for, has been produced by the way in which sexually based hierarchies are described in a good deal of recent feminist writing.

For example, in Hartmann's formulation, the reorganization of households under patriarchical control was decisive in the petty accumulation that accompanied the development of capitalism. Yet, she argues, since those relations apparently still exist — that is, since a good deal of production still takes place privately in homes and the labor force is rigidly organized on the basis of sexual hierarchies — it is correct to conclude that patriarchy, while not necessarily universal, occupies a much broader historical niche than does capitalism.(33) Hartmann's conclusion flows directly from her earlier insistence that women's subordination expresses the same relevant set of relationships, whether it occurs in late feudalism or advanced capitalism. But my point is that its relatively longish history is an artifact of Hartmann's conceptual tools rather than evidence of its independence from different modes of production.

Eisenstein offers a slightly different argument. Patriarchy, she states, does not change by virtue of the economic system within which it operates, but because of its own internal dynamics. Yet, she argues:

There is a continuity to patriarchical history that has not existed
in economic history. [Patriarchy is] a term that expresses the
continuity of women's oppression, which has existed through
different economic systems.   Patriarchy is not as historically
specific a system as any economic system we have known. It
changes historically but universal qualities of it are maintained
even if they are specifically redefined.(34) (My emphasis)

In short, for Eisenstein there are aspects to patriarchy that are
immune to historical dynamics — even its own. This immunity is what
gives the domination of women by men its special force.

Eisenstein's arguments are similar to many of those offered by
recent feminist writers who accept history as mere chronology rather
than define it as the study of the social forces responsible for bringing
events into the world, reshaping them, and eventually causing their
demise. Historical change (which is what we mean by history) occurs
when social structures (sexual hierarchies and economies, for example)
are brought into new and entirely novel relationships with each other,
so that in the process they lose their original identity and result in
fundamental changes in the entire society.

CONCLUSION

I began by suggesting that the effort to construct a theory of women's
subordination that avoids both economism and biologism has resulted in
the construction of central analytic categories equally amenable to the
determinist explanations offered by some biologists. It is the existence
of these commonalities that allows for the observation of anthro-
pologist/sociobiologist Lionel Tiger that much feminist thought is
reconcilable with a sociobiological explanation:

I've already noted the feminist answer [to why male dominance
exists]: patriarchy exists because it has existed for so long and
so universally. Despite enormous variation in standard of living,
religious belief, economies, political history, ideology and kinship
systems of different societies, the same pattern broadly prevails
because males have always dominated females in an effective
and widespread scheme. . . . If male dominance extends over the
whole species — and has existed for so long — we seem con-
strained by the law of parsimony to look first into the biological
information and theory at our disposal for an explanation.(35)

I have not been interested in documenting empirical inaccuracies in
the feminist writings I have been referring to. Quite to the contrary. I
believe that the majority of them have brilliantly drawn our attention
to crucial aspects of women's existences that have previously remained
outside of what was perceived as the legitimate preserve of social
scientific investigation. Nevertheless, the effort to avoid identifying

women's social and political subordination with imperatives of the economic system has been purchased, in my view, at an enormous price. New life has been breathed into old stratagems of biological reductionism.

I want to be quite clear that I do not think the feminist writers I have been referring to are biological determinists. What I do believe, however, is that what they construct out of the descriptive tactics I have explicated here is a kind of phenomenon that can be easily imported into the biological frame of reference.

1. Both sociobiology and the feminists I have referred to treat the occurrence of male dominance as the same sort of social phenomenon, whether it is found in advanced capitalism or socialism or feudal societies. In that sense, male dominance, or at least fundamental aspects of it, exists apart from the particular constellations that compose the society and distinguish one social formation from another.

2. Both sociobiology and some forms of feminist thought consider the phenomenon in question — sexual hierarchy — apart from its particular form in any given society. Male dominance, distinguished from the way it is manifested, becomes the object of theoretical inquiry.

3. From the viewpoint of the two theoretical frameworks, male dominance as such continues to exist quite apart from the social and historical processes whereby one kind of society is replaced by another. Therefore, within both these frameworks, the history of male dominance is merely a temporal trajectory from its origins in some distant past to the present, rather than a set of historical processes. But it is these historical processes that are responsible both for bringing male domination into being and for fundamentally revising it as a social phenomenon when social structures change. From the viewpoint of sociobiology as well as of the kind of feminist theory I have been discussing here, male dominance exists in social time, but core aspects of it are essentially untouched by the social forces that have structured historical time into discrete and identifiable historical moments.

The way these feminist writers have raised the question I have been discussing has encouraged the tactics they have adopted: Why has male dominance existed over the course of so many centuries? I am not entirely clear how to answer that question — partly, I am sure, because of my own limitations. But I suspect the other problem is that it is not the right question, at least to begin with.

I think we must begin by understanding why such a widespread lack of equality has characterized the entire world economy and what structures, processes, or forces have created, sustained, and reshaped inequalities in response to the contradictions to which they are so evidently subject. Once we have some broad answers to those questions, we may be in a better position to investigate inequalities between men and women within the social fabric in which they have occurred.

Unpaid domestic labor and childbearing and rearing — the roles assigned to women and the roles to which socialist-feminists direct their theoretical and political attention — are one form of social labor that shares important features with a myriad of other activities. Here I have in mind subsistence cropping, informal marketing (in our time, the flea markets and garage sales that dot uban sidewalks and rural front yards), informal exchanges of services (rides to work and child-care exchange, for example), and the multiplicity of other activities that are nonwaged and subordinated to those more conventionally defined as part of the economic system.

Women rather than men perform the majority of such nonwage domestic labor. Nevertheless, before inquiring into why this kind of work has been so disproportionately parcelled out to women, we must first have some firm idea about the nature of the activities and how they fit into the general scheme of things. Absolutely hindering such investigations are notions of patriarchy, the descriptive tactics that generate them, and the kinds of research they invariably lead to. Many theorists – indeed most feminist theorists who would define themselves as socialist feminist – have used the apparently different forms of labor to argue that they represent two distinct kinds of systems, one capitalist and the other patriarchal. Here, for example, is Hartmann's position:

> Over the next twenty years, while there will be some change in the sexual division of labor resulting from conflict and struggles, patriarchy will not be eradicated. Despite at least a century of predictions and assertions that capitalism will triumph over patriarchy – a situation in which all production would take place under capitalist relations and all people would be wage earners on equal terms – patriarchy has survived. . . . This means that a substantial amount of production will remain in the home. . . . It is necessary . . . that a substantial proportion of women's collective work hours be retained in the home if the patriarchical requirement that women continue to do housework and provide childcare be fulfilled.(36)

Eisenstein, as well, explicitly contrasts nonwaged activities with those that are waged. To her, the former are patriarchal in form and the latter capitalist. She argues that while each is shaped by the other, their pristine nature is best captured in the two different forms of activities each organizes:

> capitalism has a set of controls which emanate directly from the economic class relations of society and their organization in the workplace. And it seems to assume a harmony between the two systems at all points. As we move further into advanced capitalism we can see how uneasy this relationship is becoming. As women increasingly enter the labor force, some of the control of patriarchal familial relations seems to be undermined – the double day becomes more obvious. But the ghettoization of women within the labor force at the same time maintains a system of hierarchical control of women, both sexually and

economically, which leaves the sexual hierarchy of the society intact. Deference to patriarchal hierarchy and control is shown in the very fact that the search for cheap labor has not led to a full integration of women into all parts of the labor force.(37)

Ironically, by attempting to escape economism, a good deal of feminist theory not only has employed tactics compatible with biological determinism, but has left economism virtually unscathed. By insisting that the world is composed of two relatively autonomous systems of social relations that come in contact with each other and are ultimately intertwined – one organized around the public economy and the other around the private world of reproductive labor – feminist scholars implicitly accept the position they initially and rightly attempted to criticize. By constructing noneconomic and transhistorical explanations for women's subordination, they permit relations of production to be the only ones that apparently are attached to the principal motors of history and reshape the rest of the social world.

Young makes an observation parallel to the one I am offering when she notes that dual-system theory "tacitly endorses the traditional Marxian position that the 'woman question' is auxiliary to the central question of a Marxian theory of society."(38) Yet I doubt that one must supplant Marxism with a new kind of "feminist historical materialism," as Young goes on to suggest, to bring the women question into central consideration.

It is true that until very recently Marxist analysis has stressed the historical processes by which capital begins to be able to assert its control over the surplus labor time of workers by removing a substantial portion of labor from the home. But it is not necessary to Marxism to then conclude that any labor which escapes this direct domination is by that fact either outside of capitalist relations or auxiliary to it. The world capitalist system is composed of a multiplicity of labor forms that were brought into being by the full development of capital – no matter how much they may resemble earlier forms. It is hardly anti-feminist to suggest that a woman in her kitchen, who depends on her husband's wage and thus his goodwill, is in a situation no less determined by the processes that compose the world capitalist system than is an unemployed male Black worker in Detroit, a female Black subsistence farmer in southern Africa, or a white male fully employed computer technician in Menlo Park. The task is to discover the processes that create these divergent, yet ultimately united patterns of labor relations.

To be sure, Marx pointed out over a century ago:

In all forms of society there is one specific kind of production which predominates over the rest, whose relations thus assign rank and influence to the others. It is a general illumination which bathes all the other colors and modifies their particularity. . . . In the Middle Ages, capital itself – apart from pure money-capital – [had a] landed proprietary character. In bourgeois society it is the opposite. Agriculture more and more becomes merely a branch of industry, and is entirely dominated by capital.(39)

Similarly, in an earlier period, such as feudalism, family-centered relationships of male power and authority cast their long shadow on all other relations, even those that were increasingly outside their sway. While nonpatriarchal forms of production were being organized, they continued to pay obeisance to the traditional structures of authority and control.(40) In our own period, by contrast, patriarchy is merely present in what Marx would call its stunted form.(41) But that is not to argue that the subordination of women is not a part of, or even inherent in, other social forms.

To be true to the feminist mission and understand the contemporary relations between men and women in ways that can lead to fundamental changes, feminists must be prepared to explain how and why such historical processes take place and how and why old forms of domination are supplanted by new ones. By asserting the existence of a system of social relations theoretically immune from capital, although empirically caught up in it, we ignore the presence of that process and its effects on our lives.

The key problem is to first confront the multiplicity of labor forms that comprise the world capitalist system and the ways they have been brought into relation with wage labor. What I suspect we will find when we begin to consider capitalism as the unity of contradictory elements is that unequal and hierarchical gender roles, along with other kinds of systemic inequalities anchored in nonwaged relations, play a fundamental role in holding those contradictory elements together in a unified system.

By identifying essential features of contemporary gender roles with antediluvian relations between men and women rather than with the wide variety of current inequalities that comprise the social world, feminists are in very real danger of adopting a theoretical framework that is incapable of taking seriously the various nongender specific forms of oppression.

NOTES

(1) Judith Stacey, "When Patriarchy Kowtows: The Significance of the Chinese Family Revolution for Feminist Theory," in Zillah Eisenstein, ed., Capitalist Patriarchy and the Case for Socialist Feminism (New York: Monthly Review Press, 1979), 299-348.

(2) Joan Smith, "Sociobiology and Feminism: The Very Strange Courtship of Competing Paradigms," Philosophical Forum XIII (Spring, 1982): 281-308.

(3) Ruth Hubbard and Marian Lowe, Eds., Genes and Gender II: Pitfalls in Research on Sex and Gender (New York: Gordian Press, 1979).

(4) Richard M. Burian, "A Methodological Critique of Sociobiology," in Arthur L. Caplan, ed., The Sociobiology Debate (New York: Harper & Row, 1978), pp. 376-396.

(5) Edward O. Wilson, "Human Decency is Animal," New York Times Magazine, October 12, 1975.

(6) Edward O. Wilson, Sociobiology: The New Synthesis (Cambridge, MA: The Belknap Press of Harvard University Press, 1975).

(7) Lionel Tiger and Robin Fox, "The Human Biogram," in Caplan, The Sociobiology Debate, pp. 57-63.

(8) Rosalind Petchesky, "Dissolving the Hyphen: A Report of Marxist-Feminist Groups 1-5," in Eisenstein, Capitalist Patriarchy, pp. 373-389.

(9) Ibid., p. 376.

(10) Ibid., p. 377.

(11) Ibid., p. 378.

(12) Iris Young, "Socialist Feminism and the Limit of Dual Systems Theory," Socialist Review 10, 2-3 (March-June, 1980): 158-169.

(13) Gayle Rubin, "The Traffic in Women: Notes on the Political Economy of Sex," in Rayna Reiter, ed., Towards an Anthropology of Women (New York: Monthly Review Press, 1976).

(14) It is important to note that Rubin uses the term "sex-gender system" to denote "a set of arrangements by which the biological raw material of human sex and procreation is shaped by human social intervention" and is therefore neutral with respect to the particular form it takes. But Rubin argues that up until the present the sex-gender system has been characterized by the exploitation of women in and by the exchange relationship between kinship groups in which men have the advantage. Rubin, "Traffic in Women," p. 165.

(15) Nancy Chodorow, The Reproduction of Mothering: Psychoanalysis and the Sociology of Gender (Berkeley: University of California Press, 1978).

(16) Ibid., p. 86.

(17) Ibid., p. 5.

(18) Ibid., p. 86.

(19) Zillah Eisenstein, The Radical Future of Liberal Feminism (New York: Longman, 1981), 21-22.

(20) Ibid., pp. 21-22.

(21) Ibid., p. 28.

(22) Eisenstein, Capitalist Patriarchy, p. 25.

(23) Heidi Hartmann, "The Family as the Locus of Gender, Class and Political Struggle: The Example of Housework," Signs 6, 3 (Spring, 1981): p. 373.

(24) Ibid.

(25) There is a growing literature on household formation and petty accumulation. See for example the following: Hans Medick, "The Proto-Industrial Family Economy: The Structural Function of House-holds and Family During the Transition from Peasant Society to Industrial Capitalism," Social History, 3 (October, 1976): 291-315; and David Levine, Family Formation in an Age of Nascent Capitalism (New York: Academic Press, 1977).

(26) Heidi Hartmann, "Capitalism, Patriarchy and Job Segregation by Sex," in Eisenstein, Capitalist Patriarchy, p. 206.

(27) My colleague Dale Tomich has drawn my attention to this crucial difference between forms of labor that aid in the early development of capital and those that are a consequence of that development. I develop this point in a forthcoming publication: Joan Smith, Immanuel Waller-stein and Hans-Dieter Ever, Households and the World Economy (New York: Sage, forthcoming).

(28) Eisenstein, Capitalist Patriarchy, p. 25.

(29) Martha E. Gimenez, "The Oppression of Women: A Structuralist Marxist View," forthcoming in Ino Rossi, ed., Structural Sociology: Theoretical Perspectives and Substantive Analysis (New York: Columbia University Press).

(30) Eisenstein, The Radical Future, p. 22. Eisenstein is careful to dissociate universality and inevitability, as would most of the other writers to whom I am referring. Nevertheless, this does not moot the point I wish to make here. In order for a social relationship to have core universal aspects, it must rest on a set of conditions that coexist with it across time. Eisenstein argues that this condition is the hierarchical sexual organization of Western society. But that is to assume that this

hierarchy (insofar as it relates to the specific architecture of patriarchy) has remained unchanged, and that it articulated with the rest of the social world in all relevant respects in the same way in 300 B.C. as it does in 1983.

(31) As noted above, none of the feminist writers I have referred to in fact explicitly endorses universality as a feature of female subordination, and several quite explicitly reject it. Even so, their frame of reference lends itself to that interpretation. On the other hand, a number of feminist writers do assert the universality of female subordination. I have not discussed their work here since it would have amounted to the construction of a "straw-woman."

(32) Michelle Z. Rosaldo, "The Use and Abuse of Anthropology: Reflections on Feminism and Cross-Cultural Understanding," Signs 5, 3 (Spring, 1980): 389-417.

(33) Hartmann, "The Family," p. 391.

(34) Eisenstein, Radical Future, pp. 21-22.

(35) Lionel Tiger, "Male Dominance? Yes, Alas. A Sexist Plot? No." New York Times Magazine (October, 1970).

(36) Hartmann, "The Family," pp. 391-392.

(37) Eisenstein, Capitalist Patriarchy, pp. 28-29.

(38) Young, "Socialist Feminism," p. 176.

(39) Karl Marx, Grundrisse (New York: Vintage Books, 1973), p. 106.

(40) Henri Pirenne, Medieval Cities (Princeton, N.J.: Princeton University Press, 1946).

(41) Marx, Grundrisse, pp. 105-106.

Figure IX. Marie and Michel Bastien, Montagnais-Naskapi of Labrador.
Photograph by Richard Leacock.

8
Ideologies of Male Dominance as Divide and Rule Politics: An Anthropologist's View

ELEANOR LEACOCK

Eleanor Leacock details the ways in which ideas of innate differences between women and men support our hierarchical social and economic system. She looks at claims that anthropological data demonstrate the existence of a universal "women's nature" and discusses the problems with such claims. To show the fallacies of these kinds of arguments, she discusses the historical contexts of patriarchy and describes some egalitarian societies where neither sex holds power over the other.

In 1514, the Italian philosopher Niccolo Machiavelli published a treatise entitled The Prince, in which he gave advice on how a prince could obtain and hold power. Since only the upper classes and their scribes were literate at that time, Machiavelli did not gloss over the crass realities as he saw them. He wrote that a prince is

> often obliged for the sake of maintaining his state, to act contrary to humanity, charity, and religion . . . [and] cannot and should not fulfill his pledges when their observance is contrary to his interest, and when the causes that induced him to pledge his faith no longer exist. . . . It is necessary that a prince should know how . . . to be a great hypocrite and dissembler . . . he should have a versatile mind, capable of changing readily, according as the winds and changes of fortune bid him. . . . [He should] swerve from the good if possible . . . [but] know how to resort to evil if necessity demands it.

Such behavior succeeds, Machiavelli stated, "for men are so simple, and yield so much to immediate necessity, that the deceiver will never lack dupes." Elsewhere Machiavelli wrote cynically, "the great majority of mankind are satisfied with appearances, as though they were realities, and are often even more influenced by the things that seem than by those that are."(1)

The forms of power have changed from princes to presidents and parliaments since Machiavelli's day, but the techniques for gaining and holding power have not. (At least not basically.) Instead, techniques for making governmental authority appear to be responsive to popular needs and opinions have been highly elaborated. As corporate profits go up, real wages go down, and inflation soars, endless committees and commissions are appointed to debate the mysteries of economic problems, and the holders of power behind the scene make good use of Machiavelli's principle that people can be more influenced by appearances than realities. In 1954, corporations furnished 28% of federal taxes, but by 1975 they had worked their share down to 12%. During that time facory workers went from paying 6.9% of their income in federal taxes to 12.8%.(2) And this when one quarter of all the people lucky enough to be working full time in 1978 were making under $5,000 a year, another third under $15,000, and only a tenth over $25,000.(3) However, through the newspapers, radio, and TV which corporate business either owns outright or controls through the buying of advertisements, it presents itself as responsible and civic-minded – you should be grateful to be "helped" by your friendly banker! People turn to TV, the movies, newspapers, and magazines for information as well as entertainment and usually do not realize how systematically they are being misinformed about the realities of their lives.

The best known Machiavellian technique for confusing people and controlling them is that of "divide and conquer." If people are divided against each other, they will not come together to challenge the power held by the rich. As long as working people are suspicious of each other on the basis of religion, nationality, race, or sex, they can be led to believe that their interests are unavoidably at odds with those of other working people, rather than with corporate business. During the 1930s, when automobile workers staged "sit-in" strikes within the factories, some raised the question, why, since workers make the cars, should the bosses own and sell them? After all, the capital of the large factory owners was built on the labor of previous factory workers. Why should not the people who actually produce the cars be the ones to profit from their sale? Divide and rule politics have succeeded in erasing such questions from the minds of workers – or most of them. Fearful for their jobs, and indeed the possibility of working at all, they see other workers as the problem. American workers are fearful that foreign workers such as the Japanese are getting "their" jobs; white workers feel threatened when Black workers call for an end to discrimination; native-born workers are suspicious of undocumented "illegal aliens;" and male workers become angry at women's demand for the right to work at equal pay.

Today it is more essential than ever for holders of wealth and power to keep people divided because the spread of literacy, the growth of communication, and the steady migration of workers from one country to another are bringing people of the world ever closer. The awareness that we live in a world that is interdependent and that "one world" can be built on the common needs and desires of working people for a decent friendly life cannot help growing. It is necessary for those in power that working people believe the assertion well taught in school and constantly pushed by the media, that people must compete for jobs if a society is to be "free." Most carefully hidden is the fact that if the United States, with its highly developed industrial plant, were organized cooperatively instead of competitively, there would be more than enough work to go around; indeed, everyone would have to work only a couple of days a week to produce everything we need.

In Machiavellian style, racial, religious, and national hate and suspicion are carefully nurtured to keep working people divided internationally and nationally. And finally, at the core of people's personal lives, they are kept divided in their own homes, divided by gender. Precisely in the area where people search for love and support, and seek a retreat from insecurity and competitiveness, they face a tangle of relationships and attitudes that all too often make the home itself a bitter battleground.

The patriarchal structure of family relations gives husbands petty power over their wives, so that men seem to benefit from the subordinate position of women. However, it is the wealthy owning and ruling class that really benefits, and in ways that are both economic and political. Economically, women, as unpaid household labor, sustain and service their worker-husbands and produce and rear worker-sons and daughters. This relieves the state from taking responsibility for the economic support of the young and the old — tasks that should be public and social, not private and individual.(4) At the same time, women who are not married or whose husbands are low-paid or unemployed furnish a pool of "reserve labor" that is moved in and out of the work force as needed. Since these women are supposedly supported by men, they can be paid lower wages than men.

Politically, women's subordination helps divide the working class in three ways. Since women must join the labor force as low-paid workers who help pull wages down, they face resentment and antagonism from working men. Yet when they and their children are dependent on the wages of individual men, this renders men more docile and fearful of losing their jobs if they organize to fight for decent wages and working conditions. And most bitter of all, women's subordination allows the frustration and anger that men should direct toward organizational action at the work place to find an outlet in the privacy of the home through petty tyranny and verbal abuse, neglect and promiscuity, wife beating and child mistreatment.

It is small wonder that some women see the fight for female liberation as a fight against men. At home they must fight their husbands and sons; on the job, their bosses or co-opted union foremen, both usually male. When they fight for their children at school or for decent medical care, male principals and doctors hold control over women teachers and nurses. And landlords and politicians are almost all men.

Here is where the media jump in and play their divisive role. The message they continually promote is that men are innately preoccupied with competition and aggression and inevitably seek to dominate women and other men, while women are naturally submissive, and, as mothers, are innately attuned to servicing and conciliating men. In sum, social life will always be highly competitive, and the best women can do is act as peacemakers to help soften some of the rough edges. Other contributors to this book discuss ways that facts are distorted by both scientists and popularizers to maintain this image. The rest of this chapter will deal with such distortions and their refutations in the field of anthropology.

There are four principal ways in which anthropological data are used to try and prove that the dominance of aggressive males over maternal and submissive females is a universal of human society caused by deep psychobiological drives. These are:

1. The assertion that the desire to dominate others through aggressive action is universal (despite the existence of societies where aggressive behavior is strongly disapproved of and very rare).

2. The assumption that society has to be either patriarchal, with men dominating women, or matriarchal, with women dominating men (despite the fact that many societies were egalitarian before they were incorporated into capitalist relations — relations between the sexes were reciprocal and autonomous, with each sex taking care of its own responsibilities).

3. The illusion that by taking jobs outside the home, women are for the first time engaging in "productive" labor, free from economic dependence on men (despite the fact that in class societies all but upper-class women are economically "productive," while in egalitarian societies women always produce about the same or more than men).

4. The assertion that ideologies of male superiority and female inferiority are universal (despite the fact that there are many societies that place equal value on women and men).

The television "spectacular," Primal Man, recently presented by the Traveler's Insurance Company and endorsed by the National Education Association offers a crass example of the first distortion.

> In the harsh order of nature, there is but one universal competi-
> tion — to survive. The secret of that struggle is dominance . . .
> the oldest game in the world. . . . Competition for leadership is
> an eternal truth of the animal world and the world of men. . . .

Anthropologists agree that humanity's ancestors were rather small, defenseless creatures, and that their survival and further development depended upon sociability and cooperation. Not so, however, according to Primal Man. On Neanderthals, our immediate predecessors, the narration stated, "family structure, leadership, and social order was still based on strength, power over the group, and possession of the females." The best hunter "established his authority and controlled a primitive pecking order: a hunter over other men, men over women, and youthful strength over age."

When a Neanderthal hunter "moved on," the commentary continued, he took "his weapons, his woman, and his son." A girl child "was part of the family only as long as she could keep up." The image that accompanied this bizarre statement (for who would reproduce the group?) was of a little girl, unable to climb over a boulder and sliding back, exhausted, while her mother, without a backward glance, dutifully plods on behind father and son. That archaeological data show that Neanderthals lived in friendly multifamily groups and cared for their infirm (as evidenced by skeletons of people disabled by accidents who lived on) was of little interest to the producers of this show. Instead, the script intoned, "the Neanderthal hunter, the dominant male, moved brutally into the future. . . ."

Within the academic world, assertions of male dominance may be more elegantly phrased, but they are no less stereotyped. The sociologist Steven Goldberg, whose book The Inevitability of Patriarchy is subtitled on the dust cover "why the biological difference between men and women always produces male domination," argues that the reason is greater male aggression associated with the hormone testosterone.(5) The sociobiologist Edward Wilson asserts incorrectly that provisioning by men while women "stay home" is universal and therefore probably genetically based. His protege, David Barash, argues at length that the double standard for sexual behavior is biologically determined.(6) Nor is there any lack of anthropological statements about universal male supremacy.(7) Perhaps most influential are those of the eminent French academician, Levi-Strauss. Instead of arguing for male superiority, he takes it for granted. Seeing human society as "primarily a masculine society," he builds a theory of social origins on women as virtual "commodities" exchanged in the "transactions" of "male operators."(8)

Despite such expert testimony, data have always been available to show that egalitarian relations between women and men have existed in many cultures, and that if anything, they are more "natural" than the relations of dominance and subordination found in stratified societies. Even those who argue for universal male supremacy have to concede that people who support themselves (or did until recently) by gathering wild vegetable foods, hunting, trapping, collecting wild animals, and/or fishing and collecting sea foods, were generally peaceful and non-aggressive, placed a high value on cooperation and good humor, and were characterized by far greater female independence and equality than societies dependent on agriculture.(9) Societies dependent on gathering and hunting are closer than other cultures to the way our ancestors lived for millions of years. As people have moved away from direct ties with the rest of nature, the trend has been toward greater and greater male dominance and aggression, not less. So much for male dominance and aggression as major "natural" governing drives.

An increasing number of anthropologists, including myself, are presenting the evidence that there was parity between women and men in most gathering-hunting societies or are collecting new data in field studies that focus on women's activities and viewpoints instead of ignoring them. My own field work in 1950 and 1951 was among the

Montagnais-Naskapi, native peoples of the Labrador Peninsula, Canada. At the time I was there, the Montagnais-Naskapi still retained many features of their former independent lives as hunters and fishers, and they gave me insight into a level of respect and consideration for the individuality of others, regardless of sex, that I had never before experienced. Research into the efforts seventeenth century Jesuit missionaries made to convert these people to European lifestyles and teach them European principles of male authority in the family and of chiefly authority in the band, further illustrated the equality of the sexes that existed among the Montagnais-Naskapi. Only recently, under the combined influence of missionaries, fur traders, and government officials, has this equality begun to change.(10)

Colin Turnbull has documented the absence of female subordination in a gathering-hunting society in a very different part of the world, among the Mbuti of Zaire. Turnbull lived with the Mbuti and witnessed the joint planning and carrying out by women and men of their collective hunt, the ceremonies emphasizing the interdependence and autonomy of the sexes that dissipated potential tensions between them, and the "authority and power" held by elder women. An older woman "may be a gentle, loving, and kindly old lady one moment," Turnbull writes, but when a dispute arises and she comes into the center of the camp to criticize, "in a flash she becomes pure power and is heeded by everyone."(11)

A classic monograph by Radcliffe-Brown on the Andaman Islanders off the east coast of India suggests many similarities with Mbuti culture and also refers to the authority of female elders.(12) However, since Radcliffe-Brown wrote little about Andamanese women, research into other accounts of these people is needed to reconstruct women's roles and gender relations among them before their lives were disrupted when India colonized the island. Fortunately, gender relations among another gathering-hunting people in that part of the world have been carefully studied. Agnes Estioko-Griffin and Bion Griffin worked with the Agta of eastern Luzon in the Philippines, some of whom are not very far removed from their former way of life, and found them to be fully egalitarian. Women are economically independent, hunting if they choose to, as well as gathering vegetable foods. They control the distribution of the foods they acquire, sharing them within the group or trading them outside, and participate as actively and vocally in group decision-making as do men. There is no double standard for sexual behavior, and in addition to occasional instances of polygyny (the cowives usually are sisters), the Griffins found an instance of polyandry, a woman living with cohusbands.(13)

The native peoples of Australia, former gatherer-hunters now fighting to maintain a measure of independence on their own lands and to work on ranches and in the cities without being discriminated against, have been much studied by anthropologists. While no one questions the economic importance of women who provided more than half the daily diet, it is usually argued that men exerted authority over them by asserting ritual superiority and threatening them with physical violence. Increasingly, however, women anthropologists have been looking at Aboriginal Australian society from the women's point of view and have been revealing another side to the story. Frustration, drunkenness, and violence are indeed problems among Aborigines, subject to racism, genocide, and violence against them.(14) But women are not cowed by male violence. A woman may leave a husband who beats her, fight back, rally her relatives in her defense, or herself initiate a fight with her husband. As for Aboriginal culture, while men have their secret rituals, women have theirs. Some rituals are jointly carried out. All are important. Furthermore, women often have their own section of the camp, where some may live and others may visit, but which is taboo to men. There they share and exchange food, socialize, rest, and conduct their sacred rituals. Today, as they see their traditional rights being undermined by the patriarchal practices of the Australian state, Aboriginal women are beginning to organize in their own defense.(15)

Balanced gender roles that were equally important economically, socially, and ritually, also existed among many village-living farming cultures – or did before they were changed by the colonial expansion of Europe. The Iroquois, natives of New York State, are the best known example. According to the sexual division of labor, women did the gardening, gathering, and food processing, and controlled the distribution of food and other goods that were stored at the ends of the multifamily "long houses." Men were responsible for obtaining meat and fish and for defense. Both participated in ritual life. Women elders appointed the "sachems" who were responsible for negotiating intervillage affairs and relations with outsiders, but the policies they enacted were decided upon by both women and men.(16) A variety of comparable arrangements existed among other North American Indian farmers, with women controlling a large part of the economy and sharing in religious life and social and political decision-making. Contrary to the opinion of some anthropologists and historians, women who chose to and had the requisite abilities became political and military leaders responsible for relations with outsiders.(17)

Research is making clear that in many parts of the world male chiefs were appointed or backed up by colonial regimes to replace political arrangements in which both women and men played a part. This is particularly the case in Africa, even in those areas where some inequality between the sexes was developing in connection with state organization and other social inequalities. In these societies, it was not unusual for kings and "Queen Mothers" to share responsibility and authority at the highest levels, while councils made up of females and males or separate female and male associations organized various aspects of economic and social life at the village level.(18)

As can be seen, such social arrangements are neither matriarchal nor patriarchal in the sense of one sex holding power over the other. Instead, gender roles are balanced and reciprocal. The work of each sex is recognized as essential, and the conditions and products of that work are controlled by the sex that carries it out. Women are not dependent on individual wage-earning men, and children are seen as ultimately the responsibility of a larger unit than a nuclear family. Thus, children do not suffer economically from the divorce of their parents, although divorce is usually easy and at the desire of either partner.

What led to the development of patriarchy is an important question. I have elsewhere elaborated on the proposition made by Engels in The Origin of the Family, Private Property, and the State, building on the work of Morgan in Ancient Society, that the inequality of women was related to the development of inequality, generally, that resulted from the specialization of labor and trade. If I may quote myself:

> Networks of exchange relations were originally egalitarian in form, for profit was not involved. However, the production and holding of goods for future exchange created new positions and new vested interests that began to divide the commitments of some individuals from those of the group as a whole. The role of economic intermediary developed and separated the process of exchange from the reciprocal relations that had bound groups together. Concomitantly, the holders of religious and chiefly statuses, traditionally guardians of produce that was redis-tributed as needed, acquired novel powers from the manipulation of stores of locally unavailable and particularly desirable merchandise. . . . The seeds of class difference were sown when people began to lose direct control over the distribution and consumption of the goods they had produced. Simultaneously, the basis for the oppression of women was laid, as the communal kin group became undercut by conflicting economic and political ties. In its place individual family units emerged, in which the responsibility for raising future generations was placed on the shoulders of individual parents, and through which women's public role (and consequent public recognition) was transmuted into private service (and loss of public esteem).(19)

Exactly how did all this take place, and why were women the op-pressed sex? These questions are being examined by feminist scholars, some of whom are looking at the beginnings of female subordination in what are called "ranking" cultures and others at its later stages in urban, class-based, and state-organized societies.(20) The proposition I am exploring at present is that women became doubly exploited because they were doubly exploitable, both as producers of goods and as producers of labor itself. As work became "alienated" — as it changed from a person's self-directed activity that produced goods she or he would use or exchange into activity for a social sector that had gained the right to commandeer labor or its products directly or hire labor in exchange for goods or money — the significance of women's reproduc-tive capacity changed entirely. To produce people as people and perpetuate society was a matter of status and pride, but to produce people as labor that served an upper class became an economic burden and social disability. This did not happen quickly, and as African data in particular show, women organized to defend their status. However, the shift from kin-based collectives to individual families as economic units ensured male complicity and eventually undermined the ability of women to protect their interests.

In any case, whatever the processes involved and their variations in different historical and geographical circumstances, the point is that patriarchy developed. It is a matter of history and not of biology or psychology. Today multinational corporations are its primary bene-factors as women around the world are increasingly drawn into wage labor as underpaid workers without the benefit of support services to help maintain their families.(21) It is ironic at a time when from one-third to one-quarter of the world's households are estimated to be female-headed and female-supported that female dependence in nuclear families is being so strenuously asserted as "natural." Far from natural, female subordination is at the center of a system that continues to enable a wealthy few to benefit from the poverty of many, hemming them in by patriarchal laws, practices, and attitudes. Communication has become elaborated beyond anything imaginable in Machiavelli's day, but the dominant message remains the same: "divide and rule."

NOTES

(1) Howard Becker and Harry Elmer Barnes, Social Thought from Lore to Science (New York: Dover, 1961), Vol. I, pp. 304-305.

(2) "New Tax 'Reform' Act: Rich Still Get Richer," The Guardian, Oct. 13, 1976: 4. (Statistics taken from the Wall Street Journal and the Bureau of Labor Statistics.)

(3) Andrew Hacker, "Creating American Inequality," The New York Review, Mar. 20, 1980: 21.

(4) The concept of public social support should not be interpreted to mean support in institutional settings that are segregated.

(5) Steven Goldberg, The Inevitability of Patriarchy (New York: William Morrow, 1973).

(6) David Barash, Sociobiology and Behavior (Amsterdam: Elsevier, 1977).

(7) For examples, refer to Eleanor Leacock, "Women in Egalitarian Societies," in Renate Bridenthal and Claudia Koonz, eds., Becoming Visible, Women in European History (Boston: Houghton Mifflin, 1977), pp. 16-18.

(8) Claude Levi-Strauss, "The Family," in Harry L. Shapiro, ed., Man, Culture and Society (New York: Oxford, 1956), p. 284; The Elementary Structure of Kinship (Boston: Beacon Press, 1969), p. 117; The Raw and the Cooked (New York: Harper & Row, 1970), p. 276.

(9) Elman R. Service, The Hunters (Englewood Cliffs, NJ: Prentice Hall, 1966).

(10) Eleanor Leacock, "Montagnais Women and the Jesuit Program for Colonization," in Mona Etienne and Eleanor Leacock, eds., Women and Colonization, Anthropological Perspectives (New York: Praeger, 1980).

(11) Colin Turnbull, The Forest People (Garden City, NY: Doubleday, 1962); "Mbuti Womanhood," in Frances Dahlberg, ed., Woman the Gatherer (New Haven: Yale University Press, 1981); "The Ritualization of Potential Conflict Between the Sexes Among the Mbuti," in Eleanor Leacock and Richard Lee, eds., Politics and History in Band Society (Cambridge: Cambridge University Press, 1982).

(12) Alfred R. Radcliffe-Brown, The Andaman Islanders (New York: Free Press, 1964), pp. 47-48.

(13) Agnes Estioko-Griffin and P. Bion Griffin, "Woman the Hunter: the Agta," in Frances Dahlberg, ed., Woman the Gatherer.

(14) F. S. Stevens, ed., Racism: The Australian Experience (New York: Taplinger, 1972), Vol. II, Black versus White.

(15) Ruby Rohrlich-Leavitt, Barbara Sykes, and Elizabeth Weatherford, "Aboriginal Woman: Male and Female Anthropological Perspectives," in Rayna R. Reiter, ed., Toward an Anthropology of Women (New York: Monthly Review Press, 1975); Diane Bell, "Desert Politics: Choices in the 'Marriage Market'," in Mona Etienne and Eleanor Leacock, eds., Women and Colonization; Diane Bell, "Women's Business is Hard Work," Signs 7 (1981): 314-337; Diane Bell and Pam Ditton, Law: The Old and The New, Aboriginal Women in Central Australia Speak Out (Canberra: Aboriginal History, 1980).

(16) Eleanor Leacock, Myths of Male Dominance (New York: Monthly Review Press, 1981), pp. 237-240; Peggy Reeves Sanday, Female Power and Male Dominance (Cambridge: Cambridge University Press, 1981), pp. 24-28.

(17) Robert Steven Grumet, "Sunksquaws, Shamans, and Tradeswomen: Middle Atlantic Coastal Algonkian Women During the 17th and 18th Centuries," in Mona Etienne and Eleanor Leacock, eds., Women and Colonization. For brief accounts of other North American egalitarian horticulturalists, see Eleanor Leacock, Myths of Male Dominance, pp. 237-246; and Alice Schlegel, "Male and Female in Hopi Thought and Action," in Alice Schlegel, ed., Sexual Stratification, A Cross-Cultural View (New York: Columbia University Press, 1977).

(18) Annie M. D. Lebeuf, "The Role of Women in the Political Organization of African Societies," in Denise Paulme, ed., Women of Tropical Africa (London: Routledge and Kegan Paul, 1963).

(19) Eleanor Leacock, "Women in Egalitarian Societies," in Renate Bridenthal and Claudia Koonz, eds., Becoming Visible: 31.

(20) In addition to previously cited works, I would add here Karen Sacks, Sisters and Wives, the Past and the Future of Sexual Equality (Westport, CT: Greenwood Press, 1979), and Christine Gailey and Mona Etienne, eds., Women and State Formation in Pre-Industrial Societies (New York, Bergin, 1983).

(21) "Development and the Sexual Division of Labor," Signs special issue (Winter, 1981), Vol. 7, No. 2.

Figure X. Tongan Woman Painting <u>Ngatu,</u> a stenciled and decorated form of Bark Cloth. Photograph by Peter Carmichael, courtesy of William Collins Publishers, London and Christine Ward Gailey.

9
Origins of the Sexual Division of Labor *

LILA LEIBOWITZ

Lila Leibowitz proposes an interactive, biosocial model for the origins of the division of labor by sex. She presents evidence that early hominids did their work in ways that were not sex-specific. With changes in diet and in the technologies of food acquisition and processing, individuals needed to learn different skills in order to perform the more complex tasks, and skills became differentiated by sex. Now children get sorted long before reproductive sex differences make their appearance and are socialized for the tasks they will perform as adult women and men. In this model, technological, social, and biological developments go together, and there is no point asking simplistic questions about which comes first. A fundamental conclusion of the model is that the subordination of women did not accompany the appearance of a sexual division of labor and thus is not something basic to the human condition.

INTRODUCTION

The "common sense" explanation of the division of labor by sex that is usually offered is that it is related to differences in size and strength between early, proto-human women and men and to the lengthened "biological" dependency of the young. This implies that the sexual division of labor is protocultural and, therefore, "natural." But this notion does not bear up under close inspection. In this article I will try to show that early hominids of both sexes, despite their differences in size after reaching sexual maturity, engaged in the same kinds of productive activities. Adult females just combined these activities with bearing and nursing the young.

The explanation of the sexual division of labor offered here is built around three main points. They are as follows: 1. The quintessential human adaptation is the invention of and reliance on production. The elaboration of productive processes, followed by the differentiation of various kinds of productive activities, are preconditions for <u>organizing</u> production. A regular sexual division of labor thus was unnecessary as long as production was unspecialized and undifferentiated. 2. With the

*I would like to express my gratitude to Nathaniel Raymond, Ruth Hubbard, Alan Klein, Ellice Gonzalez, Carolyn Fluehr-Lobban, Stephanie Coontz, and Peta Henderson for reading and commenting on an earlier draft of this chapter.

123

emergence of technological innovations which led to the development of a number of different productive processes, divisions of labor became practicable. While the division of tasks along sex lines was influenced by the different reproductive functions of women and men, the division of labor itself was a social construct that arose out of new techniques of production. 3. Firm rules and the institutionalization of a sexual division of labor arose in conjunction with the regularization and expansion of Exchange between groups. (I will use "Exchange" with a capital "E" to refer to moving goods between groups, and "exchange" with a lower case "e" to refer to what took place within groups.) The expansion of Exchange was made possible by the new technology and was regularized by incest prohibitions, contractual marriages, kinship designations, and family arrangements, all of which are linked to the establishment of formal rules for the sexual division of labor. All are the products of cultural processes. None are part of our "natural" legacy.

The evidence I use to support this explanation is necessarily indirect. Two major pieces of that evidence come from biology. The first has to do with the fact that whereas early hominid males and females who were sexually mature were markedly different physically (e.g., sexually dimorphic), life expectancies were short. Sexually reproducing, physically differentiated adults rarely survived for any length of time. Consequently many foragers were young and physically undifferentiated by sex.

The second biological datum has to do with the fact that the size differences between females and males diminished recently and rapidly. After eons during which the size difference between females and males was marked, this sex difference was reduced during the period when fire and projectile hunting techniques became widespread. Since dimorphic and nondimorphic species have different mating patterns, this physical change seems to indicate that mating patterns were transformed as production became complex. Evidently Exchange assumed great importance at this time and marriage contracts and kinship systems became vehicles of political and economic transactions. "Family" became part of the social landscape and the sexual division of labor was institutionalized.

I deal only generally with the archeological evidence that testifies to the simplicity of early foraging techniques and make little mention of sites used by early humans which have been interpreted by the archeologists Glynn Isaac as "home bases." These sites have been characterized as places where females and dependent youngsters spent much of their time while adult males foraged. Richard Potts has analysed the detritus at such sites and the length of time they were used (five years or so).(1) Comparing that detritus with what is found at the temporary campsites of contemporary foragers, he concludes that the sites were not "home bases" but may have been "safe" places to which game was brought again and again by groups of foragers. The foragers ate the meat raw and scavengers consumed what they left, a very different pattern than that found at recent sites. Potts argues that genuine, human home bases were not likely to have evolved prior to the controlled use of fire and suggests that the notion of a "home base" has become entrenched in human evolutionary theory only because the idea of home or community is central to modern life.

THE BASIC DATA

Most people assume that the sexual division of labor is derived directly from biological differences between the sexes that are expressed in sexual dimorphism, even though the cross-cultural and anthropological data indicate otherwise. Let us briefly look at this evidence.

All human societies today have some sort of division of labor along sex lines; that is to say, all of them have arranged matters so that there are some tasks men are supposed to perform regularly, and others that fall into the category of women's work. Societies differ a good deal, however, with respect to how labor is divided between the sexes. Nearly any anthropology text offers up a list of societies in which Western notions of what women and men are supposed to do are overturned. What actually happens "on the job" and in daily living adds further variety. There are societies where anyone, regardless of sex, is expected to do almost, but not quite, everything that needs to be done, at times alongside members of the other sex, at times segregated from them. There are also cultures where nearly every conceivable task has been designated as either women's work or men's work. How strict such designations are also differs by time and place. Under different circumstances, a man who performs what a society designates as women's work may attract no attention at all, may be subtly ostracized or openly punished for his actions, or may be honored in one way or another. Much the same difference in responses to women who pursue men's activities is documented in the anthropological literature. That cultures differ greatly in how much they separate what women and men do, and how strictly they observe and maintain these distinctions is not as well recognized as the fact that women's work in one society is often men's work in another.

Why, then, do people in general and many scientists still regard the sexual division of labor as directly derived from biological differences?

Despite all the variability the fact remains that all known human societies have some sort of division of labor along sex lines. Furthermore, the biological differences between women and men are universally recognized and recognizable. Though physical differences between human females and males are not as marked as they are in some other primate species, and although one can find women who are taller, hairier, or more muscular than some men in their own population and than all men in some other population, humans are nevertheless members of a sexually dimorphic species. This "universality" of biological sex differences plays a part in how the origin of the "universal" division of labor by sex is viewed. Some theories hold that the physical differences between women and men provide the basic reasons for dividing productive work. Others regard these physical differences as merely a set of conditions which were taken into account when the techno-cultural innovations that encouraged a division of work roles emerged, when the advantages of dividing labor were recognized, and when the habit of dividing labor by sex was institutionalized.

THE TWO BASIC MODELS

Theorists who have built models of early human situations agree on at least one point. All assert that underlying any division of labor is the concept – or practice – of exchanging goods,(2) and underlying any exchange of goods is "production." Production implies that individuals actively get or make a good in greater amounts than they plan or are able to use in order to provide others with that good.(3) They agree that "exchange" is any situation in which people who do or make certain things provide others with a good, and the others reciprocate either by returning the same good at another time or by returning some other good immediately or later. However, the models they build differ regarding how "production" arose. Two basic models of the origin of production are discernible.

Biodeterminists argue that exchange arose because the biological differences between females and males result in different natural propensities or different activity profiles. As a consequence, the sexes produce different things. Typically, the model says that women (as well as primate and hominid females), because of their physical characteristics or their "natural" or normal involvement with pregnancy, nursing, and/or care of the young, were inclined and ultimately required to refrain from certain subsistence activities, usually collecting game.(4) Men's biological traits, on the other hand, encouraged them to pursue these activities and the game. Men brought in meat, and women brought in vegetable foods. The outcome of the "natural" sex-differentiated subsistence activities resulted in the existence of producers who produced different products. This situation then generated the need to exchange products. In biodeterminist models, the habit of exchange emerged because of differences in products, and the sexual division of labor existed prior to the emergence of Exchange.

Many Marxists, as well as other sociologically-oriented theorists, suggest explicitly or (more often) implicitly, a somewhat different sequence of events. They indicate that both production and Exchange must have been in place well before a formalized division of tasks or products along sex lines. The variability of incest rules that regulate mate Exchanges and the variability of rules governing the way labor is divided in recent human societies leads them to conclude that the bases of such rules are social and cultural. Their analyses result in a model in which the sexual division of labor, incest taboos, marriage, kinship and kin groups all emerged to cement alliances and to sustain intergroup Exchanges of products and people. Sociological models, therefore, suggest that sex-undifferentiated production and a distribution of products preceded within-group exchange, and that Exchanges of some sort between groups preceded the invention of the sexual division of labor and of sex-differentiated production or products.(5)

The sequence of events sociological analyses implicitly postulate is roughly as follows. First, the habit of production appeared; that is, individuals, both female and male, pursuing similar or identical subsistence activities began distributing to those around them what they did not themselves consume and began consuming what others had produced. Reliance on each other led them to produce goods deliberately for distribution and to engage in what anthropologists call generalized reciprocity. Later, when and if people moved or production exceeded local needs, intergroup Exchange occurred if the opportunity offered itself. I will argue that as it became advantageous to Exchange products, skills, or personnel, a sexual division of labor was institutionalized along with incest rules and marriage rules to maximize those advantages, and as a consequence, within group exchange was regularized.

From a sociological perspective, a satisfactory biosocial model of the evolution of the sexual division of labor should begin by explaining the ways in which evolving hominids of both sexes became producers rather than self-feeders; then it should show the ways in which exchanges (or Exchanges) of products and/or of people arose; and only in its last phase need the model deal with the origins of the sexual division of labor. I have not yet seen such a model.

SHARING AND PRODUCTION

The two most familiar explanations of why and how production came about do not deal directly with the concept of production but focus instead on sharing, and do so in a manner that I consider biodeterminist. The discovery that sharing is practiced by some chimpanzees and baboons, who take game and either give out pieces of meat or eat side by side on a carcass, is the basis of one such explanation. Primate hunting, though it occurs only in a few settings, is cited as the kind of protohominid behavior that must have given rise to production for distribution and exchange. The way these primates forage for game is tied to the sexual division of labor on the grounds that male baboons and chimpanzees take game more frequently than females do and expend more time and energy on taking game.(6) Yet the data in fact show that chimps or baboons who take game — whether female or male — do not spend much time on this activity and don't get to eat much meat. In other words, game collecting and meat eating are rare and meat sharing is even rarer.(7)

Viewing meat sharing as the basis for production seems questionable on several grounds. For one thing, social predators far from the primate line, and whom no one implicates in "production," often share meat in a social setting. Lionesses and wolves even bring game back to their young, which is more like "production" than anything chimps or baboons have been seen to do. Furthermore, the basic staples of primate foragers, human and nonhuman, are plant foods. Among nonhuman primates, those that forage side by side rarely share the fruits or roots they collect. Nevertheless individuals of both sexes have been seen to share such vegetable foods in response to gestures of request,(8) and nursing mothers have been seen to give bits of vegetable foods to their infants.(9) The notion that production for exchange derives from the habit of sharing meat is based on confusing a sustenance behavior found among many predators with a human activity that is qualitatively different and exaggerates the role of males as providers of meat. Some versions of this male-centered "sharing" model argue that the most successful male hunters are also the most successful impregnators who spread their "hunting genes" around as they give out game. This notion is not borne out by the data regarding sexual activities among hunting chimps or baboons.(10)

A less popular, feminist rather than masculinist, biodeterminist version of the origins of production for exchange and of the sexual division of labor credits plant-collecting females with inventing "sharing."(11) This explanation of the origins of the human "habit" of production states that mothers (e.g., females) began to share by giving their infants food, then began to gather enough food to give some to their older children (inventing carrying devices in order to bring back enough plants for them), and eventually began giving some of what they had gleaned to males in exchange for the meat the males had collected. Aside from the fact that primate males have been observed sharing vegetables as well as meat,(12) this model, which calls for the transformation of maternal generosity and sharing into production for distribution raises some practical questions: Why didn't males gather whatever vegetable foods they needed while they were out hunting, as they do routinely in foraging societies? Why didn't mothers systematically collect small game, as they do among the Tiwi, and skip the exchange with men entirely, as they do among the Hadza?

In essence, both kinds of biodeterminist models assume sharing as the basis of production. They develop out of the notion that sex differences in activities somehow existed as soon as our primate or proto-human ancestors began going after game and resulted in an intrinsic sexual division of products. Production is confused with sharing, and sharing becomes the province of one or the other sex. Both models stem from the view that physical differences dictate sex differences in behavioral and productive capabilities. However, the data do not support this generalization. Production, as we shall see, seems to have arisen under circumstances in which sex differences were of secondary importance. Among primates, sexual dimorphism does not mandate different tasks for females and males, though it permits males and females to engage in the same activities in slightly different settings, thus minimizing competition for resources.

DIMORPHISM AND WHAT IT TELLS US

It is relevant to this discussion that while there is a good deal of debate about how to classify early hominid remains and whether all of them belong to a single species, there is an emerging consensus that the early hominids who walked on two legs were not only small – adults were only 3½ to 5 feet in height – but that they also exhibited marked sex differences in size.(13) By the time Homo erectus types appeared, the height of members of the line leading to Homo sapiens had increased. A strong size dimorphism is still found in early Homo erectus populations. Male-female size differences diminish only in late Homo erectus populations.   For two million years, sexual dimorphism in height remained marked while hominids became taller.(14)

Despite many claims to the contrary, the presence of physical sex differences tells us little about social patterns. Size differences between the sexes among living terrestrial and semiterrestrial primates do not, in fact, correlate with any particular form of social organization and do not correlate with pairing arrangements.

Dimorphic primates live largely terrestrial or semiterrestrial lives. Species in which males are larger and have bigger teeth than females exhibit a variety of social organizations. Chimpanzees live in large amorphous and variously organized populations.(15) Baboons live in a variety of settings, such as forests and savannahs(16) and exhibit different patterns of social organization in the different places.(17) Groups of Patas monkeys include females who tolerate one or two males, while among hamadryas baboon groups a male may be found "herding" females.(18) Among orangutans, where dimorphism is extreme, each female with her young occupies a range. Males are "loners" and usually travel widely over several such ranges. Yet orangs raised in captivity and returned to "the wild" become social, aggregating, tool-using apes.(19) In Sumatra, where small siamangs chase male orangs from food, these orangs ally themselves peacefully with a female for a while. In Borneo, where logging operations are displacing orang populations, lone males attack and "rape" females.(20) Even parenting is variable. In some troops of Barbary Apes (who are actually monkeys), males have been observed carrying and caring for infants, while in other troops this has not been seen to occur.(21) Male Rhesus monkeys are rarely involved with infants in the wild, but turn out to be capable of concerned parenting in laboratory settings.(22) Behaviors vary, but among all these primates provisioning others is not tied in with dimorphism. Individuals generally rely on feeding themselves. A sexual "division of labor" simply does not occur. In dimorphic species, in which different populations or groups do different things, it is eminently clear that the behavior is malleable, adaptable, and learned, and that the particular social form it takes is shaped by circumstances and experience. The "fact" of sexual dimorphism among early hominids by itself cannot, therefore, be translated into conclusions about specific forms of social organization. Clearly many types of organization are possible, as they are among other dimorphic primates, and many have occurred.

Does the occurrence of sexual dimorphism have anything to tell us about the social interactions of primates? The answer appears to be that it does. Despite the variability of the social arrangements among sexually dimorphic terrestrial primates, several biological and behavioral conditions that are characteristic of all of them suggest an explanation. First, in all these species dimorphism becomes marked only at puberty, when males continue to grow and females usually become pregnant and slow down or stop growing. Secondly, this dimorphism occurs in conjunction with a reproductive cycle that makes adult females rarely available for insemination; females who are pregnant for many months and nurse for several years are out of the mating pool for long periods of time. Thirdly, the adult males usually range more actively and widely than do encumbered adult females. (This sex-difference in the size of ranging areas is not characteristic of nondimorphic arboreal primate species.)(23) These three conditions create a pattern of circumstances that leads to the differential distribution of mating opportunities among males.

The outlines of the pattern are the following. Females become pregnant for the first time soon after puberty, stop growing, and experience a decline in activity levels. From then on, there are long intervals between successive fertile periods. The activity levels of males are usually very high during their adolescent growth spurt and for a while thereafter. As the males become larger and otherwise differentiated from females, the males' food needs are quite high. Particularly in terrestrial settings, growing males tend to find them-selves competing for food with other animals, especially with females who are pregnant or nursing and also eating for growth, though not their own growth. Healthy, growing, active males who are experiencing a growth spurt usually wander widely, presumably at least in part to satisfy their hunger. (In some places, where adolescent males move away from the group, they begin to find foods females rarely eat.) If a male who wanders widely grows big, avoids or intimidates predators, and survives, he is obviously in a position to bump into a female (or two or three) who is in one of her infrequent fertile periods. A male who is not as active and/or fails to survive the trip obviously has fewer mating opportunities. The hungry, growing, active male is more likely to father an infant (who, if male, may inherit a tendency toward the same growth pattern) than his less fortunate peers. As he ages, his activity levels decline, and his mobility may be reduced. Nevertheless, the longer he lives the more infants he will have a chance to father. Obviously, more mating opportunities are open to large males who are spurred to wander and manage to survive their wanderings than to smaller males. (The fact that a male's growth and maturation rate affect his reproductive success is documented in a dimorphic species of deer in the only study to date that clearly identifies each newborn's biological father).(24)

By contrast, all the females have the same kinds of mating opportunities, even though those who tend to be smaller apparently have a long-term reproductive advantage over larger females. (Data that will be reviewed below indicates that where the quality or quantity of food is a problem, females with lighter nutritional needs come to sexual maturity earlier, are in better health, and have more and healthier babies than their sisters.) Whatever the adult size of a female, she inevitably can find mates, often "transient" ones, during her rare fertile periods.

Evidently, a major size difference between the sexes of a terrestrial primate species tells us only one thing about its social interactions: that the females who survive to maturity have similar mating opportunities, whereas among males, mating opportunities vary in that active males who tend also to be bigger have a reproductive advantage over other males. Having big males serves the species well. It allows the males, who are engaging in the same kind of food-getting activities as the females to get more food by "going abroad" for it. This removes some of the foraging pressures on females.

A RECONSIDERATION OF GROWING UP HOMINID

Sex differences in size tell us little about early hominid social organization. Does the evolutionary fact of an overall increase in size among early hominids indicate anything about changes in hominid social arrangements?

It is commonly (and incorrectly) believed that the larger the size of a primate species, the longer it takes for the members of the species to mature sexually, and the longer the young are in a state of dependency. From this we might be tempted to conclude that the increase in size of hominids indicates that the maturation period of hominid youngsters grew longer and longer by degrees as one generation replaced another. Such a conclusion is unwarranted.

Leakey's and Prost's casual observations on Zinjanthropus,[25] as well as Mann's systematic analysis of the extensive Swartkrans fossils[26] indicate that some early hominids (Australopithecines) matured at a rate closer to that of present-day human populations than to that of present-day large primates. Early hominids took about as long to reach sexual maturity as we do. Among our sexually dimorphic ancestors, the small females, Mann estimates, became sexually mature around the age of twelve (and pregnant presumably shortly thereafter) if conditions were right.

Startlingly, Mann's analysis of over three hundred fossil specimens leads him to the conclusion that the average age of death among Australopithecines was also around twelve, though McKinley's analysis of the data suggests an average life span of about twenty years.[27] Despite the different life expectancy figures, which reflect different estimates of infant mortality rates, a similar population structure is suggested by both analyses. Assuming, as both Mann and McKinley do, a somewhat shorter birth interval than the four to five year spacing found among present-day chimpanzees, a female who had a first infant around twelve, had another at about age fifteen, and another about three years later, and so on. Like the males of her generation, who perhaps fathered one or another of her offspring, she probably died before all her young were sexually mature. A few individuals of both sexes presumably lived into their thirties. What can we conclude from this?

It is all too easy to interpret the population profile that emerges from this pattern of late sexual maturation, early death, and high mortality rates as one overflowing with orphaned youngsters, handicapped by the loss of their mothers. Let us brush aside our biases about the dependency of human children and our preconceptions about the skills and information they must acquire before they become fully functional adults and look again.

Given what we know about dimorphic primates, savannah groups of these early hominids would have been constituted of a small number of fully adult large males (who presumably circulated widely between groups), a similarly small number of infrequently fertile adult females (most or all of them with infants and small youngsters), and a rather large number of "orphaned" females and males at different stages of prereproductive physical development. Individuals who were orphaned while young and prereproductive had to forage for themselves or cooperatively to survive. The situation resembles one that has been observed in a population of vervet monkeys, where it was found that throughout the period of study, mortality was high and the birthrate low in three groups. "Family size [sic] was small and there was a large number of orphans. . . . All of the animals spent the greatest proportion of their days feeding and foraging."(28)

Among the early hominids, presumably the physically similar males and females were able to forage in much the same ways. Since hominids have survived, we must assume that many of the orphaned youngsters succeeded in surviving to a reproductive age — that is, to 12 years or older. Only then did the females become less wide ranging by virtue of pregnancy and the encumbrances of infants. Only then did some of the males become large and likely to move about more widely than within the confines of a group.

Both males and females had by age 12 experienced a long learning period in a group large enough to insure their safety. For some, neither parent had been around for a long time. Before reaching maturity many must have been called upon to forage for themselves. If, in fact, an individual's mother lived long enough to produce a half or full sibling, mother's attention probably was diverted to the new infant. Under such circumstances she was as likely to benefit from what the young forager found as the other way round, a situation that Tanner envisions in her model of early gathering societies.(29)

A division of labor is present if those who are encumbered or incapacitated are treated as nonproducing consumers. Such a division of labor may well anticipate dividing labor in other ways, such as, along lines that generate differentiated products. Tanner notes that, "The common assumption that it [a division of labor] was primarily or exclusively by sex is, however, an oversimplification."(30) The character of the age distribution data in early population suggests that dimorphism played an insignificant role in differentiating foraging activities by sex. It also suggests that maximum cooperation (generalized reciprocity) was important for survival.

It can be inferred from another set of biological data (see below) that first pregnancies probably did not occur immediately after puberty, that adult females had only a few successful pregnancies, that births were more widely spaced than Mann and McKinley propose, and that the survival of an infant or youngster depended on the cooperation among group members.

Frisch's recent researches on body fat, puberty, and fertility in modern human populations indicate that three factors influence human fertility: the amount of food individuals get, the kinds of food they eat, and the amount of physical activity in which they engage.(31) Modern human populations differ from other primate populations not only in their furlessness, but in the fact that though men and women are not very different in size, women, unlike other primate females, develop permanent deposits of breast and buttock fat upon becoming adult. Let us deal with Frisch's data on females first.

Frisch found that the age at which puberty occurs and the maintenance of a regular menstrual cycle are correlated with the proportion of a woman's body weight that is invested in fat. Under-nutrition slows body growth, delays the time at which puberty occurs, and reduces fertility in females. Starving women stop menstruating. Underweight, malnourished and (surprisingly) obese women become amenorrheic; that is, they do not menstruate. How much and what is eaten as well as levels of physical activity together determine how much fat a woman carries. Very active women on a poor or marginal diet stop menstruating; on a healthy but marginally weight-sustaining diet they do not menstruate while nursing infants. The birth weight of an infant is correlated with the pregnancy weight of its mother, and an infant's survival is correlated with its birth weight. Consequently, an ill-fed, very active woman has few healthy children.

In males "severe undernutrition results in loss of libido, a decrease in prostate fluid, a decrease in sperm motility and longevity, and, eventually, the cessation of sperm production, in that order. Under-nutrition ... delays the onset of sexual maturation in boys."(32) Fur-thermore, high rates of sexual activity reduce sperm counts (something men who are "sexual athletes" may or may not realize). In addition, aging has a deleterious effect on quality as well as quantity of sperm. Finally, and far from unimportant with respect to early hominids, Frisch notes that experimental evidence drawn from laboratory animals indicates that substituting fat calories for carbohydrate calories hastens fat deposition and sexual maturation in males as well as in females. Frisch's data are relevant here and will also be significant in the analysis of later events.

Now, let us return to our populations of early hominids. The archeological evidence indicates that some of them were taking small game (thus adding animal proteins and fats to their diet) and making simple tools somewhere between 2.9 and 2.7 million years ago.(33) What helped these predominantly youthful populations to survive, reproduce, and achieve the slow but steady increase and dispersal that characterizes the early hominid evolutionary grade? What allowed individuals of either sex to leave a genetic legacy in a population with a high mortality rate among the young, a "late" age of sexual maturation, infrequent mating opportunities, rare successful pregnancies, and a low birth rate? How were populations so at risk of extinction able to survive, replace members, and eventually expand their numbers? Apparently by inventing "production."

"PRODUCTION" FOR SURVIVAL

Many of the important actors in the scenario I see emerging from this configuration of circumstances are the females and males between about 4 and 12 years old. They were feeding themselves, but not yet sexually mature. While their range of sizes reflected the age differences among them, males and females of the same age were similar in size and body form, though adults were dimorphic. Remains in ancient sites and evidence from contemporary human foragers and other primate groups suggest that these males and females engaged in several kinds of foraging activities. Such activities at present rarely involve distinctions between what females and males (or young or old) are called upon to do. They include: 1. individual foraging for small game and vegetables; 2. group hunting (of either the surround or drive type or of the "chase and exhaust" variety) focusing on small animals; and 3. killing or scavenging large animals that are, somehow, incapacitated. These foraging activities could have been accomplished with simple tools by young foragers and by adults. (At present, adult females as well as males are known to participate in these kinds of activities.) Such individual or cooperative activities – undifferentiated along sex lines – become production whenever more is acquired than can be consumed "on the spot" and the surplus is distributed for later consumption. Production proved to be advantageous for all the actors in the scenario.

Here is how recent biodeterminist evolutionary models of behavior might explain an "instinct" for production and exchange. The survival values of production and of giving away goods without expecting an equal or immediate return for them (a form of Exchange called "generalized reciprocity") can be looked at as "genetically selfish" and a result of "kin selection." In sociobiological terms, individuals are geared toward maximizing their genetic legacy. Achieving sexual maturation as early as possible and in good health is, therefore, an "advantage" sought by the individual. Diversifying food supplies and getting as much meat to eat as possible would help achieve this advantage. Both are easier for the individual to accomplish if she or he belongs to a wide ranging, cooperating group. Presumably the individual should strive to assure him/herself that an opposite sexed individual also survives to sexual maturity. Provisioning peers of the other sex is therefore worthwhile. Provisioning same-sexed peers is also worthwhile, not only because of the rewards of reciprocity, but because the chances are high that among those same sexed peers are half siblings or "cousins" who carry some of the individual's genes. Helping feed one's own mother or caring for any of her other offspring would serve to enhance the chances of some of one's genes surviving, though one may never reach sexual maturity. Provisioning older adults, whatever their sex or relationship, pays off in another way, too. The older, more experienced members of the community are the repositories of nongenetically transmitted information useful for one's own survival. While helping each other stay alive and eat well is particularly important for orphans "trying" to reach a reproductive age, anyone who helps another is bound to maximize the chances of his/her genes surviving, and since the populations are so small, everybody is more or less related to everybody else.

While the above "explanation" makes it clear that production increased the survival chances of early hominids, it does not validate the view that "genes for production" became prevalent because of kin selection. For one thing, kin selection is irrelevant in small populations in which all or most are kin. For another, discriminating between degrees of relatedness in distributing largesse would seriously jeopardize the survival of a species barely able to replace its members. For yet another, nonkin based reciprocity rather than what is called kin-selection is evident elsewhere among animal species.(34)

To sum up, then, it appears that undifferentiated "production," or "provisioning others," or "generalized reciprocity" — or whatever one wants to call it — must have played a part in maintaining the small, youthful populations of early hominids whose marginal replacement rates kept the species hovering precariously on the edge of extinction. Inventing production evidently improved their ability to survive and even permitted a very gradual increase in numbers. The slow rates of population growth and dispersal of hominid populations indicate that replacement rates remained essentially unchanged for eons.

THE EMERGENCE OF EXCHANGE BETWEEN GROUPS

The functions and effects of dividing labor and of Exchanging as well as exchanging products have received enormous attention ever since the Enlightenment and will not be examined here. The model being explored here departs from commonly held views about the origins of exchange primarily in seeing Exchange between groups as an economic arrangement that emerged <u>before</u> the sexual division of labor was institutionalized and that standardized exchange within groups. Sociological analyses of the often arbitrary ways in which tasks are divided along sex lines usually point to the part played by the sexual division of labor in helping cement the bonds of Exchange networks.(35) Whereas Durkheim clearly says that the sexual division of labor emerged as an instrument for cementing intergroup bonds,(36) few other sociologists are so explicit. The notion that the practice of the sexes exchanging goods within groups was a precursor of a sexual division of labor, and one of the conditions that led to regularizing it, is either implicit or (as is evident in Parsons' works(37)) absent. Two lines of evidence suggest that Durkheim was correct, and that Exchange arose before the sexes were committed to exchange.

The cultural evidence suggests, that in the populations we have been discussing, males and females gathered food in the same ways during the period in which subgroups of the population began Exchanging goods. The artifacts and food detritus associated with early human groups show little change for nearly two and a half million years. These remains reflect the use of foraging techniques that are simple, involve both sexes, and call for similar activities on the part of both. The cultural evidence, therefore, indicates that the foraging activities of female and male producers remained undifferentiated for a long time.

Though foraging patterns apparently did not change much for two and a half million years, a gradual increase in the population took place as evidenced by its dispersal over an ever-widening area. Ranging more widely and producing and distributing diverse foods probably helped increase survival rates, but the extreme slowness of the rate of population growth in the face of a somewhat improved diet indicates that reproductive rates remained low. According to Frisch's analysis, maintaining high activity levels acts as a brake on female fecundity. Data supporting her analysis shows that women who lead sedentary lives become pregnant more quickly, give birth more often, and have more children than women who are highly mobile and engage in strenuous activities.(38) A low reproductive rate consequently supports the idea that during the time that foraging tools and techniques remained essentially simple, women's activities remained strenuous, and women, like men, spent little time at the so-called home base sites of this period. The maintenance of marked sexual dimorphism in the populations indicates further that no change took place in the way mating opportunities were distributed among males. There are, then, several reasons for concluding that foraging activities were not differentiated along sex lines and that mating arrangements remained essentially amorphous during a period in which intergroup Exchange (as evidenced by finds of rocks and food remains at places distant from their sites of origin) emerged as an opportunistic practice.

How and why did intergroup Exchange emerge? Dispersal and local specializations in technology and in the food products that became more diverse must have set the stage for intergroup Exchange. The wider dispersion of the slowly enlarging populations resulted in localized groups, loosely articulated to each other, with different resources, and skills that were perhaps becoming differentiated. The exchange of products differing from one locality to another, or of products that are temporarily scarce in one area probably emerged as an extension of productive patterns. It seems clear, therefore, that the habit of Exchanging products arose before female and male products and production activities had become differentiated.

THE INSTITUTIONALIZATION OF THE SEXUAL DIVISION OF LABOR AND THE EXCHANGE OF SEX-DIFFERENTIATED PRODUCTS

The reasons I believe that a sexual division of labor, along with incest taboos and marriage Exchanges, appeared late – that is, well into Homo erectus times – is based on three lines of evidence. The first involves the appearance of fire hearths and fire-hardened spears, followed by stone tipped spears, atl atls, and bows and arrows. Let us reconstruct the consequences of this transformation in hunting technologies.

Projectile hunting created new conditions. It permitted a major increase in the amount of meat in the diet of what soon became a rapidly proliferating and quickly spreading human population. Innovations made it possible for hunters to shift from an early concentration on taking a few middle-sized and larger herd animals, to taking more middle-sized and smaller animals with solitary habits.(39) How game was pursued changed. Injuring or killing game from a distance calls for sustained quiet as the pursuer stalks an animal. One or a few individuals can bring in good-sized animals to feed a number of others. Furthermore, projectile hunting tools can be used as defensive weapons against cornered game and predators, making it safer to hunt alone or in small groups. The hunters themselves had to change. The techniques of projectile weapon hunting demanded both training and self-control. Earlier technologies had called upon large groups of unskilled individuals of all ages to help with surrounds, drives, or chases; the participants saw much action, and it was useful if they made a lot of noise. By contrast, projectile hunting calls for silence and stealth and demands skill, experience, patience, and strength. These tend to be attributes of older individuals. Projectile weaponry would seem to have changed the character of the hunt in a way that transformed children or youngsters from active participants into dependents. In populations that were living longer, the youngsters' roles as primary producers declined.

Another consequence of the introduction of projectile weapon hunting was the elaboration of processing technologies that were fire and hearth centered. Thick skinned, medium-sized game posed problems. Preparing and cooking the products of the chase became time consuming. Other new activities emerged that required skill and experience: processing skins and hides, converting them into clothing and carrying devices, and making hunting equipment and the tools to process food and hides. Setting up and maintaining the shelters cum workshops where all of these activities took place were even more demanding. The new skills and techniques needed for the hearth bound activities required training and experience. Consequently, the time it took to become a fully productive participant in progressively more elaborate social activities expanded. The young became "dependent" on fully productive adults for the first time. The invention of projectile hunting weapons and the control of fire established the underlying conditions for dividing labor by sex and by age.

The complexity of these tasks was a significant factor in dividing labor and broadening the scope of the generalized reciprocity obtaining within camps or groups. Not only did this complexity call for the teaching of skills to youngsters, it put a premium on making sure that the skills and knowledge of the disabled or elderly were not lost. The aged and incapacitated, whether or not they were able to undertake hearth tasks, became indirect producers by virtue of being repositories of information. The new techniques created distinctions between the activities of the young and unskilled, the adults who could venture forth and bring back necessary supplies, and the knowledgeable elderly or incapacitated members of the community who could perform hearth bound processing tasks and the socially important job of transmitting information. While a division of labor along sex lines was ultimately an outcome of the complexity of the new technology, the initial effects of this complexity must have been to encourage dividing tasks by ability and age.

The diversity of environments that human populations came to occupy by the Upper Paleolithic indicates that foraging and processing tasks differed from place to place in technical content and social form. Hearth-oriented tasks and fire itself must have differed in importance for groups and communities scattered across the Eurasian and African landmasses. Surely Siberian foragers who hunted mammoth relied in different ways on fire and developed a different repertoire of hearth tasks than African foragers in the warmer climates who had a richer and more varied flora and fauna to exploit. With the emergence of Mesolithic technologies in communities that exploited the resources of shores, lakes, rivers, and seas, even greater variability of foraging and processing tasks – and the way they were organized – must have developed. Which tasks were assigned to what class of persons un-doubtedly depended in part on local circumstances and in part on local traditions. Whatever the way the division of labor was institutionalized, the need for dividing tasks ultimately derived from the emergence of new foraging techniques and strategies and from the new processing problems that arose from them.

The observed population growth provides the second line of evidence that suggests that the emergence of a sexual division of labor is related to the appearance of this complex of social and technological innova-tions. The increase in consumption of meat and animal fats apparently contributed to a marked increase in female fertility as well as to increased longevity. But the increase in the birth and survival rates in addition seems to reflect a behavioral change. It is obvious that those adults who did not go out on a stalking type hunt must have assumed the responsibility for performing hearth-centered tasks and for overseeing the activities of the "dependent" youngsters excluded from the hunt. Women with nursing infants presumably were nonhunters for variable lengths of time. Perhaps very pregnant women joined them. Engaging in time-consuming, hearth-centered activities involves a degree of "sedentism." Sedentism is associated with increased female fertility and with higher birth and infant survival rates. The population increase may, therefore, reflect a change in women's activities. The increase suggests that women in earlier settings, which were not complex enough to generate a sexual division of labor, were not as hearth bound or sedentary as the women in those later cultures where sophisticated forms of projectile hunting were practiced. In the latter cultures, people probably engaged in a "casual" or circumstantial division of labor that to some extent followed sex lines.

The third line of evidence that suggests that the sexual division of labor was institutionalized as projectile hunting developed and hearth activities became complex has to do with the decrease in sexual dimorphism. The size differences between the sexes are large in the Early Upper Paleolithic, but approximate the smaller modern differences by the Mesolithic. This change suggests that in the latter period small males for some reason were getting a chance to mate that they had not enjoyed earlier. (Other analysts have argued that this decrease in size differences came about because the "safer" or more specialized hunting techniques were advantageous for smaller males.(40))

Together all three lines of evidence suggest that practices that equalized male mating opportunities accompanied rules institutionalizing the sexual division of labor which were related to the expansion of Exchange and the emergence of rules governing the choice of spouses.

How and why are reduced dimorphism and the institutionalization of the sexual division of labor linked to Exchange? A casual arrangement whereby hunters hunt and nonhunters undertake hearth tasks does not constitute an institutionalized sexual division of labor, even if the majority of nonhunters happen to be women, and most or all of those going on hunts are male. Allocating the responsibility of supervising the activities of older children to women, who are engaged in tasks that permit them to assume that responsibility, more nearly approximates the institutionalized division. Still, there is something missing. Even though mothers, occupied with new hearth skills, probably found themselves involved with their youngsters for much longer intervals than had previously been the case, hunters also assumed responsibilities toward the young. In addition to providing foods that mothers and children normally did not produce, they must have taken on the responsibility for transmitting their hunting skills to youngsters. The sexual division of labor not only designates which productive tasks men and women pursue: it allocates the responsibilities for socializing youngsters into those tasks differently to men and to women. When fully articulated, the division calls for recognizing early who will be a "mother" and who will not, for deciding which set of skills a youngster is most likely to use as an adult, and for training the youngsters accordingly. In this way, girls and boys, as well as women and men, are distinguished from each other. Girls learn their skills from women, boys from men. By the time hunting and hearth tasks had become time consuming and skill based, the activities of all males and females, young and old, were differentiated, and gender distinctions were in place. I would suggest that the institutionalization of such distinctions and of the rules insisting on their maintenance occurred for the following reasons.

One aspect of the interdependence between the sexes that emerged was the _need_ for the exchange of the different products the sexes provided. This sort of exchange resembled the ongoing Exchange of different products between local groups, with one notable difference. Within-group exchange, based on a sexual division of labor, involved an inescapable interdependency. Intergroup Exchanges, while mutually beneficial, occurred irregularly and depended on when groups met, what products they had on hand, whether they needed each others' products, and whether those needs had been satisfied by previous Exchanges with other groups. Extending the inescapable interdependence of the sexual division of labor to intergroup relations can be accomplished by instituting incest rules that require the Exchange of mates between groups. Such incest rules call for formal rules governing the sexual division of labor, since they make it more likely that skills learned in one group will be of use in another.

The incest rules, which forbid taking mates from among "kin" or from among those who were members of the local group, called for groups to send skilled individuals of either sex away in contractual marriages and to attract mates into the group. Marriages established obligations and bonds and, if contracted for a long term, stabilized Exchange relationships. Marriages also made it possible to establish and maintain loose and far-flung networks of Exchange ties. The invention of incest taboos and marriage created a situation in which every or nearly every male, regardless of whether he was robust or tall or especially active at adolescence, was of potential value as a spouse if he had acquired men's skills. Similarly, a marriageable female was one who had acquired women's skills. Incest taboos and contractual marriage evidently led to the "institutionalization" of the sexual division of labor, to an equalization of male mating opportunities, and to a reduction in dimorphism as frequently monoganous unions served to stabilize and expand Exchange networks.

THE MODEL IN BRIEF: The Early Foragers

Physical sex differences between adults appear to have been quite marked in early hominid foraging populations(41). The hominids resembled other primate species in which adult males and females are physically differentiated in that their mating relationships were temporary, variable in form and content, and rarely exclusive. Foraging activities were pursued in much the same ways by members of both sexes, and there was no sexual division of labor. Adulthood appeared only after late sexual maturation (later than is characteristic of other large primates). Consequently, a large proportion of the foraging hominid population was made up of physically undifferentiated pre-adult females and males.

Sharing

The reliance on vegetable foods was nearly total at first, and, as happens among other primates with like food habits, individuals of either sex would occasionally share an item they were eating.(42) Such behavior is analogous to the sharing found among social predators and suggests that sharing was probably more usual when and where unencumbered individuals killed small animals frequently, or when they joined with others to chase and hunt small game.(43) Where taking game became a regular activity, the early hominids learned to share food regularly. Unlike social predators who also share game, these overwhelmingly youthful hominid populations had a very low reproductive rate. Populations remained small and hence risked extinction. (Populations of social predators are adequately maintained by sharing.) The development of "production," a peculiarly human social adaptation that rests on a kind of foresight not necessary for sharing, appears to have been a critical factor in hominid survival, since it made it easier for "orphaned" and incapacitated individuals to survive. Thus production contributed to sustaining a species with a low replacement rate.

Production

Production appeared when individuals or groups deliberately set out to collect goods for distribution to others. Carrying food back to "share" with others is "production." Engaging in such actions provided obvious and immediate nutritional and social rewards. The perception that "production" was worthwhile (though I doubt that its long-term survival advantages were perceived) encouraged the development of surround and drive hunting techniques that were likely to result in the capture of larger quantities of food than could be consumed on the spot.

These techniques normally called for the active participation of all able-bodied individuals irrespective of their age or sex. Many of these individuals were too young to have developed adult sex differences. Dividing labor (that is, undertaking different activities that produce different goods) presumably only occurred when immediate situations or individual circumstances called for it. Individuals, whatever their sex or physique, usually engaged in the same sorts of group or individualized foraging and hunting activities.

Exchange

The regular production and distribution of small quantities of game made animal proteins and fats dietary staples. The changed diet somewhat reduced fetal, infant and adult mortality rates, and extended life spans. The population gradually increased. Members of the sexually dimorphic species spread over an ever-widening area. Fluidly organized groups, with loose social and sexual ties to each other, became more numerous and occupied ecologically differentiated settings. Local populations found themselves producing different products. The goods produced for local distribution were sometimes Exchanged for different goods collected elsewhere or for similar goods in short supply locally. Exchanging goods increased and diversified what was available to the local groups. Production (undifferentiated by sex) continued, and in conjunction with Exchange (involving goods differentiated by locality) altered diets. The post-pubertal life span increased. The increased longevity changed the demographic profiles of successive generations. Adult height and weight increased, and the taller and heavier populations continued to be markedly sexually dimorphic.   Physical sex differences remained large over the many millennia during which foraging tools and techniques showed only slow and slight changes.

The Sexual Division of Labor and Mate Exchange

The invention and elaboration of projectile hunting tools, along with the growing use of fire, created a new and revolutionary set of conditions.(44) Following their introduction, large numbers of medium-sized game animals began to be taken regularly. Carcasses were prepared and processed in elaborate ways, and animals fats and proteins became a significant part of the diet. The accompanying population expansion is apparent in the rapidity with which groups carrying the new tool kit spread over vast areas.(45) Significantly, during this relatively recent spread of "big" game hunting, the size and skeletal difference between adult females and males first increased and then diminished to present-day levels.(46) This diminution in sexual dimorphism, occurring as it does in conjunction with the development of big game hunting (in populations that already included many adults), indicates that a radical change took place in the way the opportunities for mating were distributed. The conditions that made small females more reproductively successful than larger females, and large males more reproductively successful than smaller ones, no longer existed.   The chain of circumstances leading from the invention of projectile hunting tools to the reduction of physical sex differences includes a number of links: among them the emergence of the sexual division of labor, the establishment of rules governing mating, and the creation of more stable and extended Exchange networks. The links are articulated as follows.

Projectile hunting changed the ways in which production within a local population were pursued. Projectiles made it possible for one or a few skilled individuals to supply many people with meat from good-sized animals. Inexperienced youngsters were excluded from the new kind of hunting, but continued to engage in other kinds of foraging activities. The new game needed to be processed in time-consuming and complex ways, so that fire and hearth centered skills required considerable training and experience, just as the new ways of hunting did. Consequently, it took longer for youngsters to become fully productive adults. The ongoing responsibility for supervising "dependent" youngsters, along with hearth tasks, fell to nonhunters. As fetal and infant mortality declined, more of women's time came to be occupied with child-related tasks. The risky tasks of stalking and pursuing "big" game fell more and more often to unencumbered and skilled men. The exchange of sex differentiated products produced <u>within</u> a local population became common practice. This internal exchange firmly established the interdependence of the activities pursued by women and men and created the dependence of youngsters on adults of both sexes.

The exchange of products within groups mirrored many aspects of the Exchange of products between localities. The latter, however, lacked the element of ongoing interdependence generated by dividing tasks along sex lines. The sexual division of labor served as an instrument for stabilizing and extending intergroup Exchange networks when it was tied to incest rules forbidding mating within a localized group. Together these rules created systems of interdependence which forced groups to Exchange producers as well as products.

Projectiles are weapons against predators as well as efficient hunting tools. As projectile techniques and tools were refined, small hunting parties and ephemeral foraging groups became more common. Scattering the males and females (of whatever physique) who had acquired the appropriate sex differentiated skills through such groups and assigning them as "spouses" stabilized mating relationships. It also equalized the distribution of mating opportunities among males, irrespective of whether they were large, small, or of medium height and weight. Nearly every skilled man was of use in the mate Exchange networks. The ongoing distribution of diversified resources through these networks added significantly to everyone's food supply, and thus effectively equalized the chances of reproductive success for women with different physiques and nutritional needs. The reduction of sexual dimorphism in human populations followed. The emergence of different tasks for women and men, and presumably of gender roles with differentiated behaviors, ironically set the stage for a decrease in physical sex differences.

EPILOGUE

Physical sex differences are often regarded as the foundation on which the sexual division of labor rests. In the biosocial model outlined above, I argue that the evidence suggests that the institutionalization of the sexual division of labor created conditions that <u>reduced</u> physical sex diffferences. The model also proposes that production for distribution is fundamental to the human condition. It says that production not only preceded the sexual division of labor, but also preceded incest taboos and marriage and kinship systems. The model, therefore, departs from structuralist views that these institutions are the benchmarks of human society and define it. The model differs from the Levi-Straussian model espoused by most structuralists in another way as well. Levi-Stauss sees the Exchange of women by men as a first step in the process of "culturalization", but I argue here as elsewhere that individuals of both sexes were moved from one group to another to regularize Exchange.(47) Thus, I do not go along with the structuralist argument that women were subordinated to men as soon as "basic" cultural institutions emerged.

It is a manifestly political model. Clearly, the notion that socially transmitted innovations were crucial to the early survival of the human line has implications for our situation today when socially transmitted innovations threaten our species and all species. This model argues that innovations in social structure, not just innovations in technology, affect evolutionary events. Thus it reflects my belief that political action will play a large part in determining our future as biological and social beings.

NOTES

(1) Richard Potts, "Behavioral Reinterpretations of Lower Pleistocene Sites from Olduvai," paper presented at the annual meetings of the American Anthropological Association, December 1982.

(2) Judith Brown, "A Note on the Division of Labor by Sex," American Anthropologist 72 (1970): 1073-1078; Bernard Campbell, Humankind Emerging (Boston: Little, Brown, 1976); Euclid D. Smith, "Comment on 'Variations in Subsistence Activities of Female and Male Pongids' by B. Galdikas and G. Teleki," Current Anthropology 22 (1981): 252-253.

(3) Jules De Raedt, "Comment on 'A Marxist Reappraisal of the Matriarchate' by C. Fluehr-Lobban," Current Anthropology 20 (1979): 349-350.

(4) See, for instance, Birute M.F. Galdikas and Geza Teleki, "Variations in Subsistence Activities of Female and Male Pongids: New Perspectives on the Origins of Hominid Labor Division," Current Anthropology 22 (1981): 241-247.

(5) Lila Leibowitz, Females, Males, Families: A Biosocial Approach (No. Scituate, MA: Duxbury Press, 1978); Toshisada Nishida, "Comment on 'Variations in Subsistence Activities of Female and Male Pongids' by B. Galdikas and G. Teleki," Current Anthropology 22 (1981): 251; Janet Siskind, "Kinship and Mode of Production," American Anthropologist 80 (1978): 860-872.

(6) Galdikas and Teleki, "Variations in Subsistence Activities"; G. Teleki, "The Omnivorous Chimpanzee," Scientific American 228 (1973): 32-42.

(7) S.M. Hladik, "Comment on 'Variations in Subsistence Activities' by B. Galdikas and G. Teleki," Current Anthropology 22 (1981): 249-250; Yukimaru Sugiyama, "Comment on 'Variations in Subsistence Activities' by B. Galdikas and G. Teleki," ibid.: 253.

(8) See photograph in Teleki, "The Omnivorous Chimpanzee," p. 40.

(9) J.B. Silk, "Patterns of Food Sharing Among Mother and Infant Chimpanzees at Gombe National Park, Tanzania," Folia Primatologica 29 (1978): 129-141.

(10) Jane van Lawick Goodall, "The Behaviour of Free-Living Chimpanzees in the Gombe Stream Reserve," Animal Behaviour Monographs 1 (1968): 165-311; Thelma Rowell, Social Behavior of Monkeys (Harmondsworth: Penguin, 1972).

(11) Evelyn Reed, Woman's Evolution (New York: Pathfinder, 1975); Sally Slocum, "Woman the Gatherer: Male Bias in Anthropology," in Rayna R. Reiter, ed., Toward an Anthropology of Women (New York: Monthly Review Press, 1975); Nancy M. Tanner and Adrienne L. Zihlman, "Women in Evolution. 1. Innovation and Selection in Human Origins," Signs 1 (1976): 585-608.

(12) Nishida, "Comment on 'Variations in Subsistence Activities,' by Galdikas and Teleki."

(13) Donald C. Johanson and Timothy D. White, "A Systematic Assessment of Early African Hominids," Science 203 (1979): 321-330; Richard Leakey, "New Evidence for the Evolution of Man," Social Biology 19 (1972): 99-114.

(14) Milford H. Wolpoff, Paleoanthropology (New York: Alfred A. Knopf, 1980).

(15) Jane van Lawick Goodall, "The Behaviour of Free-Living Chimpanzees."

(16) Yukimaru Sugiyama, "Social Organization of Chimpanzees in the Budongo Forest, Uganda," Primates 9 (1968): 225-258.

(17) Thelma Rowell, Social Behavior of Monkeys.

(18) Ibid., p. 163.

(19) Gary L. Shapiro, "Reports from the Field: Orangutan Research and Conservation Project," L.S.B. Leakey Foundation News 18 (1980): 7-8.

(20) John MacKinnon, In Search of the Red Ape (New York: Ballantine, 1974).

(21) Frances D. Burton, "The Integration of Biology and Behavior in the Socialization of Macaca Sylvana of Gibraltar," in Frank E. Poirier, ed., Primate Socialization (New York: Random House, 1972), pp. 29-62; M.H. MacRoberts, "The Social Organization of Barbary Apes (Macaca Sylvana) on Gibraltar," Am. J. Phys. Anthropol. 33 (1970): 83-100.

(22) Gray Mitchell, William K. Redican and Judy Comber, "Lesson From A Primate: Males Can Raise Babies," Psychology Today 7 (May 1974): 63-68.

(23) E.D. Starin, "Monkey Moves," Natural History 90, no. 9 (September 1981): 36-44.

(24) Tim Clutton-Brock, "The Red Deer of Rhum," Natural History 91, no. 11 (November 1982); 42-47.

(25) L.S.B. Leakey and J.S. Prost, Adam or Ape (Cambridge, MA: Schenkman, 1971).

(26) A. Mann, "Paleodemographic Aspects of the South African Australopithecines," University of Pennsylvania Publications in Anthropology, no. 1 (1975).

(27) Kelton R. McKinley, "Survivorship in Gracile and Robust Australopithecines: Demographic Comparison and a Prepared Birth Model," Am. J. Phys. Anthropol. 34 (1971): 417-426.

(28) Phyllis C. Lee, "Socialization of Immature Vervet Monkeys," The L.S.B. Leakey Foundation News 23 (1982): 7.

(29) Nancy Makepeace Tanner, On Becoming Human (New York: Cambridge University Press, 1981).

(30) Ibid., p. 220.

(31) Rose E. Frisch, "Nutrition, Fatness and Fertility: The Effect of Food Intake on Reproductive Ability," in W. Henry Mosely, ed., Nutrition and Human Reproduction (New York: Plenum Press, 1978), pp. 91-122; Rose E. Frisch, "Fatness, Puberty, and Fertility," Natural History 89, no. 10 (October 1980): 16-27; Rose E. Frisch and Janet W. McArthur, "Menstrual Cycles: Fatness as a Determinant of Minimum Weight for Height Necessary for their Maintenance or Onset," Science 185 (1974): 949-951; Rose E. Frisch, Grace Wyshak, and Larry Vincent, "Delayed Menarche and Amenorrhea in Ballet Dancers," New England Journal of Medicine 303 (1980): 17-19.

(32) Frisch, "Fatness, Puberty, and Fertility," p. 20.

(33) Donald C. Johanson and Maitland A. Edey, Lucy: The Beginnings of Mankind (New York: Simon and Schuster, 1981); Science News of the Week, Oldest Tool Kit Yet, Science News 119 (1981): 83-84.

(34) J. David Ligon and Sandra H. Ligon, "The Cooperative Breeding Behavior of the Green Woodhoopoe," Scientific American 247, no. 1 (July 1982): 126-135.

(35) Claude Levi-Strauss, The Elementary Structures of Kinship (Boston: Beacon Press, 1969).

(36) Emile Durkheim, The Division of Labor in Society (New York: Free Press of Glencoe-MacMillan Co., 1974), pp. 56 ff.

(37) Talcott Parsons, "The Incest Taboo in Relation to Social Structure," in R.L. Coser, ed., The Family, Its Structure and Functions (New York: St. Martin's Press, 1964), pp. 48-69; Talcott Parsons, Societies: Evolutionary and Comparative Perspectives (New York: Free Press of Glencoe, 1966).

(38) Nancy Howell, Demography of the Dobe Area !Kung (New York: Academic Press, 1979); Gina Kolata, "!Kung Hunter-Gatherers: Feminism, Diet, and Birth Control," Science 185 (1974): 932-934.

(39) David Frayer, "Body Size, Weapon Use, and Natural Selection in the European Upper Paleolithic and Mesolithic," American Anthropologist 83 (1981): 57-73.

(40) Alice M. Brues, "The Spearman and the Archer," American Anthropologist 61 (1959): 457-469; Frayer, "Body Size, Weapon Use, and Natural Selection."

(41) C. Loring Brace, "Sexual Dimorphism in Human Evolution," in C.L. Brace and J. Metress, eds., Man in Evolutionary Perspective (New York: Wiley, 1973), pp. 238-254; Johanson and Edey, Lucy: The Beginnings of Mankind; Wolpoff, Paleoanthropology.

(42) Hladik, "Comment on 'Variations in Subsistence Activities.'"

(43) Nishida, "Comment on 'Variations in Subsistence Activities.'"

(44) Catherine Perles, "Hearth and Home in the Old Stone Age," Natural History 90, no. 10 (October 1981): 38-41.

(45) Chester S. Chard, Man in Prehistory (New York: McGraw Hill, 1975).

(46) Frayer, "Body Size, Weapon Use, and Natural Selection"; Wolpoff, Paleoanthropology.

(47) Lila Leibowitz, "Founding Families," Journal of Theoretical Biology 21 (1968): 153-169; Lila Leibowitz, "Perspective on the Evolution of Sex Differences," in Rayna Reiter, ed. Toward an Anthropology of Women (New York: Monthly Review Press, 1975), pp. 20-35; Leibowitz, Females, Males, Families.

Index

About the Contributors

DOROTHY BURNHAM is a biologist who did her graduate work at Brooklyn College. At present she is an associate professor at Empire State College of the State University of New York. She has written numerous articles, some of which have appeared in the Genes and Gender series published by Gordian Press, and in Freedom Ways magazine. In recent years, her research has focused on Black women in slavery.

ELIZABETH FEE is an assistant professor in the School of Hygiene and Public Health at Johns Hopkins University. She was born in Belfast, Northern Ireland and spent her early years traveling in South-East Asia with her Methodist missionary parents. She studied biochemistry at the University of Cambridge in England and came to the United States in 1968. As a graduate student at Princeton University, she became involved in the women's movement and wrote a dissertation on the history of scientific theories about sex and sex differences. She has since worked on the history of anthropology and medicine. Her current interests include issues in science and feminism, the history of health care, and the history of public health.

RUTH HUBBARD is professor of biology at Harvard University where she teaches courses dealing with the interactions of science and society, especially as they affect women. In recent years she has been thinking, writing, and lecturing about how the assumptions scientists make about the world influence their work and how the society in which they live influences their assumptions. She is particularly interested in the way gender – the fact of one's having grown up female or male – affects these questions. She writes and speaks on women's health issues for general audiences and is a member of Science for the People and of the National Women's Health Network.

ELEANOR LEACOCK is professor of anthropology and department chair at the City College of the City University of New York. Among her publications are introductions to Ancient Society by Lewis Henry Morgan and to The Origin of the Family, Private Property and the State by Frederick Engels, Women and Colonization (co-edited with Mona Etienne), and Myths of Male Dominance: Collected Articles on Women Cross-Culturally. Her research interests also include educational anthropology and native North American cultures. She has served on the executive bodies of the American Anthropological Association and of the Society for Applied Anthropology.

LILA LEIBOWITZ is an anthropologist and associate professor at Northeastern University in Boston. Her research interests include biosocial evolution and social structures. She has published articles in professional journals and in magazines for general readers. Her book, Females, Males, Families: A Biosocial Approach (No. Scituate: Duxbury Press, 1978), presented an earlier model of the origins of divisions of labor, which she updates in her article in this collection. At present she is working on a book that describes her research in Eastport, Maine where conflict over an oil refinery has had far-reaching effects.

MARIAN LOWE is associate professor of chemistry and a member of the Women's Studies Faculty at Boston University. She has long been interested in the social implications of scientific research, with a particular focus on the role science plays in shaping ideas about women and women's role in society. She has also worked on environmental issues, primarily issues of energy policy. Her current interests include the effects of social setting on health and the implications for women and for science of women working in science. She is co-editor, with Ruth Hubbard, of Genes and Gender II: Pitfalls in Research on Sex and Gender (New York: Gordian Press, 1979).

BEATRICE MEDICINE is a Lakota Sioux who was born and grew up on the Standing Rock Indian Reservation in Wakpala, South Dakota. She has a Master's degree in anthropology from Michigan State University and has done doctoral work at the University of Washington. She has taught anthropology at a number of universities in the United States and in Canada and is at present on the faculty of California State University at Northridge. She has published numerous articles dealing with the anthropology and politics of contemporary American Indians and is co-editor with Patricia Albers of The Hidden Half: Studies on North Plains Indian Women (Washington, D.C.: University Press of America, 1983).

KAREN MESSING is professor of genetics at the University of Quebec at Montreal and teaches courses in genetics, embryology, and the biology of women. In addition, she does research and education on reproduction and women's biology at the request of the two major Quebec unions — the Confederation des Syndicats Nationaux and the

Federation des Travailleurs de Quebec — under the terms of an agreement between these unions and the University.   Dr. Messing received her Ph.D. from McGill University and is currently researching the detection of genetic damage among workers exposed to radiation or solvents.

JOAN SMITH is a member of the faculty in the Department of Sociology at the State University of New York at Binghamton. She also chairs the Women's Studies Program at that institution. She has written extensively about contemporary social relations of production and reproduction and is currently at work on a book dealing with the growth of the so-called service economy and how women's work serves as the basis for the profitability of the industries that compose the service sector.

Lowe, Marian

WOMAN'S NATUR

Pergamon Pres

155 pages